The Horseless
RANCHER

By
Debby Schoeningh

*Hope you enjoy.
Giddy-Up!
Honda!
Debby
Schoeningh*

The Country
Side Press

Library of Congress Control Number: 2006909400

ISBN Number: 978-0-9746360-1-6

Published by The Country Side Press
P.O. Box 34
Haines, Oregon 97833

Front Cover photos by Mike Schoeningh
Cover & Book Design by Debby Schoeningh
Edited by Eloise Dielman and Joan Miller
Printed in USA by Lightning Source

To my husband, Mike, for being such a good sport and letting me poke fun at our ranching adventures. To the cows for letting me learn to be a rancher without criticizing me in public, even though I know they're snickering at the water trough. To all of my family and friends who continue to support my writing efforts and laugh along with me, and to God for allowing me to lead the life of a rancher's wife!

Special thanks to Joan Miller and Eloise Dielman for editing The Horseless Rancher, and to my mom, Helen, and son, Jake, for cheering me on.

"Ha...Ha...Can you believe it? I've got her
riding a Honda while I lay around and eat all day!"

Contents

The Horseless Rancher

Most people think that if you are a rancher, then you have cows. And if you have cows, then you are a cowboy or a cowgirl. And, if you are a cowboy or a cowgirl, then you most assuredly ride horses.

Well… all cowboys and cowgirls are not created equal. Contrary to popular belief, some of us may know which end of the horse to feed the hay to, but we have never really mastered the art of riding one. And it hasn't been for lack of trying. For the better part of 10 years I rode a horse; his name was "Asbestos." I'm not sure how he got his name; he certainly couldn't be described as hazardous material. But his unusual name did cause some confusion. Whenever the Vet sent us a reminder to get him vaccinated they would say, "It's time for Asphalt's booster."

Asbestos was a part of the ranch long before I married into it and belonged to my brother-in-law. He was the oldest horse on the place and couldn't go very fast, except when he got his nose pointed toward the barn and then he'd really take off. Well, really take off for him was more like a child running to the bathroom with his legs clenched. Actually, Asbestos never broke out of trot when I rode him. Given a chance we probably could have done quite well with a sulky in the harness races.

He was a good old boy though. When I rode him it was mostly to help gather cattle on the ranch. We usually rode toward the back of the cowherd, bringing up the rear, mainly because we were the rear. We were always pretty far behind the rest of the crew because Asbestos would have to stop about every two minutes and get a mouthful of grass. If I kept pulling on the reins to keep his head up, he would start stumbling and staggering like he'd had too many fermented dandelions while walking and grabbing bites off the tops of the grass until I would let him graze again.

Most of the time it was pretty leisurely work and was performed at this slow pace, but every once in awhile a cow would try to take off from the herd and Asbestos and I would naturally be expected to round it up and get it pointed in the right direction again.

It usually went something like this: My husband would come galloping up beside me and say, "Didn't you see that cow turn back?"

After coming out of my daydream state of wondering if I should wear my hair more like Dale Evans, I would gaze across the pasture and spot the cow and say, "Of course, we were just getting ready to take off after it, but saw you coming and thought we'd better see what you wanted first."

Satisfied, Mike would lope off and resume his place toward the front of the herd. For some reason he always made the mistake of having confidence that this dawdling duo could actually do it. I'm not sure, but it might have had something to do with him wanting dinner that night....

By the time I could get Asbestos to get his head out of the grass and pointed toward the critter in question, it was usually pretty far away. So I'd say, "O.K. buddy, it's time to move and this time we have to really go fast." Asbestos would always snort a few times, pass a little gas and start lumbering off in the direction of the cow.

Determined to not let the rest of the crew down I'd give Asbestos a swift jab in the ribs with my heels and yell, "High Ho, Asbestos." And after several swift jabs, a few slaps on the behind as well as my yelling things that the Lone Ranger probably would not have approved of, he would eventually break out of a race walker's pace and into a trot.

After several more moments of kicking and slapping I would get him into his fastest trotting pace, which by the way, for his passenger, was similar to riding a foot-high pogo stick on a gravel road – suffice to say anything that could jiggle did with extreme vigor.

It was usually about this time that I would break out into song, a little ditty I made up, which goes like this, "He's the bestos in the westos, my Asbestos." But with all of the jiggling it sounded more like a symphony of frogs with a bad case of the hiccups. Mike overheard me one time and asked if he could get me anything…like a strip of duct tape to block out the offensive noise that seemed to be coming from somewhere in my vicinity….

Anyway, after Asbestos and I would chase the cow all the way back to the pasture she had originally come from without being able to get around her, Mike would come loping up on his horse — performing his eye hiding grin that means he's not really happy with the situation, but, again, he would still like to have dinner that night — and send the cow flying back toward the herd.

Asbestos and I would soothe our egos by deciding that Mike could have never gotten the cow so quickly if we hadn't followed her into the farthest corner of the pasture through three gates and around two cattle guards and showed him where she was. Then we'd go back to the business at hand of bringing up the rear. The only problem was, by this time the rear we were suppose to be bringing up was so far ahead of us that we were more like trackers following signs of fresh cow patties to locate them again.

3

One day after spending a rather frustrating day of gathering cattle on Asbestos, I told Mike, "This horse doesn't work. I want a new one. Besides gravity is working fast enough on me, I don't need Asbestos to help jiggle everything looser."

By this time Mike had become partial to having dinner so I did get a new horse, several of them in fact, but that's another story…

Asbestos was eventually retired and lived out his last years on the ranch grazing and walking at his own pace, which was usually hard to differentiate from a stand still, but he was happy.

As for me, nowadays when people say, "Oh, you're a rancher. What kind of horse do you ride? Is it a gelding or a mare?" I reply, "It's a she and her name is Honda."

"Do you ride western or English?" they ask.

"Mostly vinyl," I say, "unless it's cold, then sometimes I will drape an old jacket over her to sit on."

"I see," they say a bit perplexed. "So, you prefer bareback?"

"Heck no," I say. "I ride her fully clothed."

Trying another strategy they ask, "Well, do you plan on breeding her some day?"

"Nah," I answer. "I may upgrade her to a 150 at some point, but I don't want anything too big or my feet won't be able to touch the ground…."

People don't give up easily though, especially horse people. Even when they eventually figure out you ride a motorcycle instead of a horse, they decide it's because you don't have one, not because you don't want one. That's also about the time they start telling you the cattle working lineage of their mare that's due to foal soon…which by the way they won't be able to keep because they have too many. And since you're a rancher, they will give you a heck of a deal…giddy-up Honda.

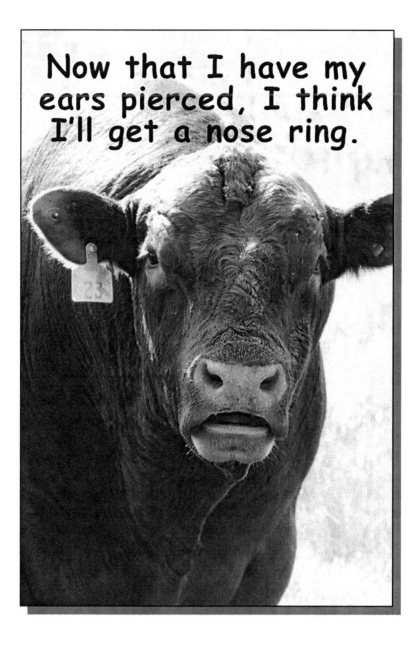

Now that I have my ears pierced, I think I'll get a nose ring.

What Color Is Your Calf Chute?

Just like other baby animals, calves are cute, fuzzy and cuddly looking, but unlike other baby animals, they have the misfortune of entering this world through a cow. That in itself wouldn't be bad, but as with all species of offspring, they have a tendency to take after their parents.

Only it's harder with calves because while they are being conniving, obnoxious and just down right ornery like their mothers, you still have the impression that they are just too cute to actually kick you or poop on your boots, so it's always somewhat of a surprise when they do.

I received my fill of the little buggers a couple of weeks ago when we branded and vaccinated them. Of all the jobs available like giving shots, branding, making steers, or even just being my husband's "lovely assistant," I chose dancing the little darlings up the bright green calf chute. I thought, "What fun! I'll get to pet them and hug them and squeeze them just like my own little bovine teddy bears."

Turns out they were more like my own little Tasmanian Devils, and guess what? They don't dance up the chute; in fact, they don't even walk up the chute. Heck, they don't even crawl up the chute — they don't want anything to do with the chute and even less to do with me.

I found out on the first group of five calves that I sent up the chute that they have an uncanny ability to turn around in a space smaller than a glove compartment. They all ran up the chute with hardly any prompting or prodding and when the first one reached the head catch, it immediately turned around and the others followed like a cascading Domino design.

Now, keeping in mind that the chute is narrow enough that I can't easily turn around in it, I had five calves trying to squeeze back by me to freedom. I couldn't move out of their way; there was no room. Since I couldn't make them all turn back around, we were at an impasse. I finally had to jump up on the chute with one leg braced on each side and let them all squirt under me.

It was then I realized I would have to walk each calf up the chute individually, and make sure its head stayed pointed in the right direction. No problem, they're small, they're cute — they're just babies for crying out loud! And pretty soon, I was, crying out loud….

I managed to maneuver one of the calves back into the chute and about halfway to the head catch, he tried to turn back on me. I gently, at arms length, tried to force his head back into the right direction. He quickly rewarded me with a well-placed kick to my shin.

It was then that my husband, Mike, replying to my string of unlady like adjectives said, "Oh yeah, I forgot to tell you that if you stand right against their back end, they won't have enough room to wind up and kick you."

So, heeding his advice, I positioned myself directly behind him. He was right, not only was I not getting kicked, I was able to use my legs to help push the calf up the chute. About the time I had the third calf up the chute using this new method, I found out that, as with all good ideas, there is usually a little "glitch," and this little "glitch" came in the form of smelly poop all down the front of my jeans. "Oh yeah," Mike said. "I guess I forgot to tell you, they have a tendency to do that."

"O.K. before we go any further," I said, "is there anything else you forgot to tell me?"

"Nah, I think that's about it," he said. "Except the crew is getting a little impatient waiting for you to get the calves up here so we can vaccinate them."

"The crew?" I asked. "Well, you and Mom will just have to wait!" Our "crew" has somehow dwindled over the years and we suspect that some of our friends and relatives may have moved out-of-town just to avoid this yearly calf branding ritual. If it weren't for the fact that moms can't say "no" to their children, we wouldn't have any help.

So the battle of the ranch wife vs. the contrary calves continued. As I pushed on their back ends they dug in and braced themselves with their front legs until their rumps went up in the air and I had to maneuver them down the chute like an out-of-control wheelbarrow with no tire. And, they continued to bless me with all kinds of offerings — kicks, head butts, toe stomps, half nelsons, and anything else they could manage to squirt, wipe or slobber on me.

Needless to say the calf chute was no longer a bright green and I was no longer in the mood to hug and squeeze the little buggers.

Finally, several hours later, as I was huffing and puffing, bruised and battered, and stuffing the last one up the chute and into the head catch, and pondering a nice long bubble bath, my husband said, "Oh yeah, there is one other thing I forgot to tell you.'

"What now," I grimaced through unruly strands of hair and a mud (we'll call it "mud" for the sake of decency) caked face.

"The crew is getting hungry — when are you going to make lunch?"

Several time spans came to mind including the one about a hot place freezing over, but I kept them to myself... after all, I had to make lunch for mom so she would help again next year.

The Cow Pokey.
Put your left
hoof in, shake
it all about...

Cows That Go Moo
in the Night

To the inexperienced, cows look like mild mannered creatures. While they are scattered throughout the countryside during the daylight hours, quietly grazing in pastures, city folks drive by and say, "Oh, look at the pretty cows. They look so peaceful and content chewing their cuds."

But ranchers know what they are really like. The fact is there is no such thing as a "real" contented cow. The only contented cows are the ones printed on the Carnation evaporated milk can because they can't kick or charge off of the label. And, if modeled after a real cow, I'm sure they were professionally retouched to "appear" more content.

But, when these conniving, controlling, and manipulating she bovines of the udder region really show their true colors is at night. And they become even more colorful during the twilight hours of calving season.

My husband, Mike, and I personally haven't slept more than three hours a night in the past three weeks. Ideally we should be able to go out and check the cows before retiring for the night, get up once in the middle of the night to peek at them, and then check them again in the morning. But it never works out that way.

For instance, just the other night Mike went out and checked the cows before we went bed and came back in and said, "Everyone looks O.K., let's finally get some sleep." The pillows were fluffed, the good nights said and just as we laid our heads down, I heard this soft, faint little noise that sounded suspiciously like a moo.

"Did you hear that?" I said. "Was that a moo?"

We both sat up in bed and strained to listen...everything was quiet. Mike said, "Nah, must be the dog. The cows all look fine tonight, go to sleep."

We lay back down again and almost caught a z when Mike bolted upright in the bed.

"Now I hear the moo, too," he said.

Again, we listen closer with the same results – not a sound.

"Well, I'm sure it's nothing," I said. "If a cow was having problems, she would really be bawling."

"Yeah, you're right. Let's get some sleep," Mike said as he lay down again. This goes on for another 15 minutes until we began to realize what it must feel like to be a windup jack-in-the-box popping up and down while the cow cranked us with her intermittent moos.

But the next time we almost got to sleep and heard a moo, it wasn't just "a" moo, it was about 20 rather urgent moos in succession, in other words she was "really bawling."

"That's it, someone must be having problems," Mike says as he jumps out of bed and into his Levis. He went out with the four-wheeler and drove through the herd shinning his spot light on each one of the little darlings only to come back and report, "Everyone is fine."

So, the next time, about 20 minutes later, she waited until we were completely asleep and started in with the bawling again.

"It sounds like the cow is right under our window," I said. "I'm going to go see what the heck is going on."

I sneaked out the back door in my terry bathrobe and pink fuzzy slippers trying not to make a sound. Even though it was really dark, I decided not to turn on my flashlight so I could catch the cow in the act and put a stop to this nonsense.

As I was feeling my way through the dark on the outside of the fence that surrounds our house, I couldn't make out the shadow of a cow anywhere. I figured she must have heard me coming and trotted off to join the rest of the heard.

So, I stepped out into the pasture a little ways for one last look and exasperated by not being able to find the troublemaker, turned around, and to my surprise walked smack dab into something big. Startled, I fumbled around and turned on the flashlight, which was pointed straight up between the two of us. When I saw the cow's eerie face in the dark with her black glowing eyes, and she saw me (I'm sure it didn't help that I had just gotten out of bed and my hair was sticking up all over), we both screamed and ran in opposite directions.

About that time Mike, hearing the screams, came running out of the house, and in my haste to get away from the big black Godzilla cow, I plowed him over.

"What in the heck is going on," he said.

"There's a big black cow out there," I screamed.

Mike, not being one to get overly excited said, "Yeah, so, there are a lot of big black cows out there."

So I told him the whole "terrifying" story of how I bumped into her and how we saw each other's faces all lit up in the dark. I then demonstrated by turning on the flashlight under my chin.

"Geez," he said as he looked at me in the dark with the flashlight on my face. "That is scary, I better go out and see if the cow's O.K. — you might have sent her into labor."

He's still paying for that one...

If you can't beat them — run!

Along the Highways
of Life

As I travel down the highways of life I have come to realize that there are certain peculiar things that I just don't understand. Oddly enough, my husband doesn't know the answers to these things either, which really surprises me, because he tells me he knows everything. But, I have also come to realize that ranchers often times fit into this same category of peculiar.

One of the things I've been considering lately because they are all over my highways of life, are the habits of quail, the funny little bird with the feathery thing protruding from its head. That in itself is worth pondering. What does it actually do? It sticks out like a radio antenna complete with its own version of the 76 gas station ball on top.

By the way, whatever happened to that 76 ball anyway? You don't see it very often anymore. I got to pondering this and had to stop and do a quick search on the Internet. Did you know there is a Web site called savethe76ball.com? The site is run by a group of people who are opposed to the company's removal of the 76 balls that are being replaced with "boring rectangular signs that aren't even orange!" I'm wondering, how did they decide to pursue this? Were they looking for a worthy cause to support and after vetoing Save the Children and Save the Earth, they decided to save the 76 ball?

Anyway, I'm getting way off the subject. That's what happens when you start pondering; it just leads to more things to ponder. The thing about quail that I really don't understand is why do they run across the highway in front of cars? They are birds. They can fly — I've seen them do this. But for some reason they insist on running in front of traffic rather than flying over it. Is it some kind of risky game of chance they play with each other or are those little antennas on their heads not tuned in to the right station?

Other birds aren't much better though. There can be an entire flock of swallows, blackbirds, or whatever, sitting around in trees and bushes beside the highway and they pick the exact moment that a vehicle comes along to fly across the highway. Even though a car only comes along on average of once every 15 minutes, they sit and wait for just the right moment. This wouldn't be too bad because, unlike the quail, they do fly. But, for some reason they only fly about three feet off the ground and right into car doors, hoods, and windshields. I know they can fly higher; I've seen them do this before too. Surely there are one or two survivors from these encounters that could warn the others, "Hey man, don't plow into those steel things with people inside, unless you want a major headache!"

Another ponderable thing on the highways of life is why do they bother to have those yellow signs that designate a deer crossing area? I have yet to see a deer cross by one of those signs. But since they do have deer crossings, I've often wondered why they don't have designated skunk-crossing areas since you see a lot more auto-related casualties in skunks than other animals. And, in between those signs they could put up signs about every 3 miles that say, "Caution, Dead Skunk in the Middle of the Road" because I'm not sure, but I don't think skunks can read any better than deer.

Feral cats are also everywhere on the highways. Cats are a little different, though, because you can usually see them sneaking up onto the highway from the barrow pit. But, at the last minute they will forget why they were going to cross the road and will turn tail and run back to the same side. Then, before they reach the side, all of a sudden they remember, turn around, and try to cross the road again. Sometimes they do this half a dozen times before you make it past them. I wonder if their indecisiveness is due to their inability to perform simple math equations. "Let's see, I've already been run over three times, that just leaves me with two more lives, no wait, I should have at least five lives left…oh, I almost forgot, there was that time I fell off the roof and didn't land on my feet…"

Cattle on the highways are also very peculiar. For instance why is it a calf will get right in front of your car and run? Most highways are at least 28 feet wide; cars are around 6 feet wide, which leaves approximately 22 feet of space for the animal to run on that is not directly in front of you. If you approach cattle and they are standing on the side of the road, inevitably a young calf will run out in front of you, and even if you try to go around it, the calf will also swerve to stay in front of you, without ever thinking, "Hey, all I have to do is step aside!" The only thing I can think of is that this is part of their early training to develop the courage to kick a dent in your fender when they become adults. I can just hear the cows giving their offspring encouragement, "That's right, honey, run. Next time you'll kick 'em good!"

Dogs on the highways are also perplexing. They continue to chase cars day after day that are obviously going far too fast for them to catch. You would think at some point, at least after a couple of years, they would give up. I wonder if dogs ever stop to think about what they would do with it if they caught one anyway. "Yeah boy, if I ever catch a car I'm going to drag it back home to chew on along with my stinky piece of year-old cat gut." I don't know… is it the smell of a car that attracts them? Maybe they would like to roll on one and then bury it…

I hate to admit it, but I'm not all that contented.

Every Cowgirl Doesn't Have to Be a Horse Girl

Just to set the record straight — Webster's Dictionary defines a rancher as "a person who owns or works on a ranch." Likewise the definition listed for cattleman is "the owner of a cattle ranch; a person who tends cattle." I did notice that cattlewoman is not even mentioned in the dictionary, which makes me wonder if Random House, Webster's publisher, gets a kick back from ranching husbands. There's where those Beef Checkoff dollars really go! But, my point is that nowhere in either definition of the words "rancher" and "cattleman" does it make reference to a horse or someone who rides one.

I mention this because I tried for years to make the horse thing happen, and as my son would say about his efforts to memorize math equations for school tests – it just didn't take!

I tried Missy, a beautiful thoroughbred mare who performed very well – in the corrals. The only problem is once I took her out of the confines of a fenced area into the pasture, apparently she thought she had been set free and forgot all about the passenger on her back. She would take off like a greyhound after a rabbit and no amount of pulling on the reins would encourage her to stop or even slow down until she was good and ready. Fortunately, she had such a smooth gait that I somehow managed to stay on. We sold her soon after buying her, but now that I'm a little older, I kind of wish we still had her. She would have offered a good alternative to plastic surgery. The G-force air current caused by her swift ride could be used to pull back and tighten the skin around my eyes.

Then there was Spot, a cute little appaloosa gelding with big gray eyes. He was the perfect size. I could get on him easily and he actually rode pretty nice — that is if I could ever get him saddled! During the brushing, bridling, and saddling process he would jump sideways, bite, kick and head butt me to the point that I was so mad by the time I got on him that I didn't want to ride any more. After about a dozen tries and several bruises later Spot became a faint speck in our memories as we sent him back to where we got him.

"Red" was a very attractive gelding, and as the people we bought him from said, "a well-bred ranch horse with lots of experience working cattle," but what they failed to mention is that you needed a seat belt to stay on him. Once he got through bucking and kicking up his heels for the first five minutes you were on him he would settle down and work cattle like a pro. I never did get on him. After watching my husband, Mike, do the bucking bronc bit, I graciously declined as in "Ain't no way I'm getting on that puppy!" He was such a nice horse in all other areas that I toyed briefly with the idea of installing side curtain airbags on my saddle, but I couldn't get my insurance company to cover him for bodily injury (my body) because he wasn't street legal.

Probably the most memorable, though, was Danny. He was a nice big quarter horse gelding and was actually my husband's horse. Mike had ridden him for several years and had him well trained, but he was still a very energetic horse. This time we approached it from a different perspective and decided Mike would train "me" to ride the horse rather than try to train the horse to "let" me ride it.

To start with Mike taught me how to lunge him in a circle on a long rope attached to his halter. For those of you new to this concept, it involves standing in one spot as a sort of revolving post while the horse goes around and around you while at your cue, going through all of the gaits, walking, trotting and galloping. Part of the reason for this is to give the horse a chance to warm up and expend some of his initial energy so he won't be overly excited when you get on. This would have worked fine, except going around and around made me really dizzy and since Danny was well trained to respond to the slightest command, having me standing out in the middle with a whip, staggering around like a drunk confused and scared him, so he began running forward and back, sideways and up and down.

Mike soon decided that I wasn't doing his horse any favors with the chaotic lunging and announced that he would take care of that from now on and I would ride Danny while he lunged both of us in a circle. Well, the walking and the trotting went fine, but when Mike asked Danny to gallop, things went awry pretty fast. When Danny went from a trot to a gallop it was a bigger transition than I had expected and I fell forward. When I fell forward I did what I thought any sensible person would do — I grabbed around Danny's neck and hung on for dear life.

Although Danny apparently didn't mind having me on his back, he didn't particularly like having me ride his neck so he stared bucking.

"Stop it, you're scaring him," Mike yelled.

"He's scaring me — make *him* stop it," I yelled back as I continued to cling to his neck.

"He thinks you're some kind of wild animal attacking him, you're going to have to let go of his neck to make him stop," Mike said as he continued to hang on to the lunge line, trying to control the bucking horse.

Finally, after what seemed like an eternity, although Mike later said it was only 60 seconds, I mustered the courage to sit up in the saddle and just as Mike said he would, Danny stopped bucking.

"O.K., let's try that again," said Mike, "and this time don't grab his neck."

"Stop the horse," I said through gritted teeth.

"When something like that happens you have to just get back on and…"

"Stop the $*!!#%! horse now," I interrupted him.

Mike signaled for Danny to stop, which he immediately did. I dismounted and walked out of the arena on shaky legs, jumped on my Honda and never looked back.

I finally conceded that although I am a "cow" girl, I am not a "horse" girl. My Honda stops when I say whoa, my Honda doesn't bite or kick me, and my Honda only bucks when I ask it to. And most importantly, my Honda doesn't leave anything for me to step in that I later have to scrape off my boots. "Good girl, Honda."

Beauty is in the eye of the beholder — and I'm mighty beholding to you.

Judging the Miss Heifer Pageant

Selecting which heifer calves to keep and which ones to take to the livestock sale is a big decision every fall, and one that isn't made any easier when the husband and wife make that selection together. I used to let my husband, Mike, pick the heifers out himself, but the last few years I've decided what this chore really needs, is my help. And I'm sure that he will concede that although I may not have the practiced eye that ranchers acquire from years of raising cattle, my help makes for a longer, more fulfilling, heifer sorting experience.

Our heifer sorting day this week began early in the morning. For some reason ranchers never think of performing tasks in the middle of the afternoon; everything has to take place at sun-up like in a John Wayne Western. But, nevertheless, I drug my weary body out of bed and took off on the 4-wheeler with the icy cold, almost winter breeze, freezing my lips shut so I could barely talk, much less crack a smile. Hey, come to think of it, maybe that has something to do with why ranchers do everything in the early morning, especially when their wives are along...

Anyway, I was opening the gates for Mike, who was driving the tractor with a load of hay to coax the cows and their offspring into the corrals, when all of a sudden I looked up at the sky and the biggest, brightest moon I had ever seen was resting on top of the mountains, and it was already daylight. Not being one to keep these amazing feats of nature to myself, I jumped off of the 4-wheeler and began pointing at the moon for Mike to see.

He kind of looked from inside the tractor cab in that direction and shrugged his shoulders and kept going. I knew he must not have seen it because he didn't act too excited so I became more insistent with my pointing. Still no response, he just gave me one of those puzzled looks that insinuated I might not be fully awake enough for the day's chore.

So out of desperation to share this beautiful sight, I finally circled my hands above my head into the shape of a big moon and pointed again. This time he looked as though he figured it out. He slammed on the brakes, got out of the tractor, and ran over to me, and with urgency in his voice said, "What is it, a dead bloated cow?"

"No, it's the moon," I said, breaking the ice seal on my lips. "If it were a dead bloated cow I would have made a circle in front of my stomach and puffed my cheeks out like this, geesh! Just look at the moon, isn't it gorgeous?"

With that he shook his head and walking back toward the tractor said, "Let's not make one of your newspaper stories out of this. We just need to get the cows in, get the calves sorted and off to the sale."

Sorry honey, I couldn't help it, I sat down at my computer and the whole "sorted" story just started coming out...

To make a long story short, we got the cows in and separated them from their calves, then we separated the good

26

cows from the bad cows. Well, let me rephrase that, I'm not sure there is a such thing as a good cow… we separated the cows that were too old, too cranky and too content to produce a calf this year from the rest of the cows.

It's always kind of sad to take cows to the sale, but they always do something to ease your mental pain like kick you on their way into the livestock trailer, which creates another kind of pain that makes you not care so much about the afore mentioned pain.

We took the culled cows to the sale and by then it was time to sort the heifers from the steers, and then finally sort out the individual heifers. So, the process began of deciding which cute little heifers get to stay on the ranch, grow up, get fat and turn into demanding, overbearing cows and which heifers are the go-to-salers. I'm sure there must be a technical name for these, but it escapes me at the moment.

As we sort through the heifers, like judges at the Miss America Pageant, we quickly get them narrowed down to 12 finalists. Then the real scrutinizing begins to pick out the six best of the 12 best. Unfortunately, they can't parade around in swimsuits or twirl batons while singing the National Anthem, so we have to rely on our keen sense of livestock savvy.

"That one has really pretty eyes," I offer. "Why don't we keep her?"

Mike scowls, "What we really need to be looking for is those that have strong straight backs and sound feet. These two need to go," he said while herding them out of the pen.

"Well, none of them are limping and they all have straight backs," I say. "Oh, there's another pretty one. Keep her."

"We don't want ones with heavy muscling; they need to look more feminine," he continues as he separates off two more.

"Like I said, pick the pretty ones!"

"It's not that easy," he said, as the Miss Heifer Pageant continues. "We also need to look at their genetics and choose ones that came from higher producing cows. The older ones would also be better because they have a higher chance of conceiving this summer." Then he ushers one more out of the pen to join the go-to-salers.

Now we're down to seven and have one more to go... He scrutinized the heifers from every angle, examining their hips and legs, and pondering their mother's history. And finally after 20 or so agonizing minutes he opens the gate and lets one out.

"O.K., that one has a nice straight back, sound legs, she's feminine and her mother is number 57, and she always raises a nice big calf," I said. "So what was wrong with her?"

He scratches his chin and pauses to think, "I didn't like her hair, it was kind of weird looking," he said.

"Like I said, just pick the pretty ones...."

Bovine yoga –
feel the stretch...

How to Snag a Rancher

It has come to my attention that there are a lot of women out there who would like to snag themselves a rancher, but aren't sure how to go about it. Ranchers are a wily lot and it takes considerable effort on a woman's part to nab one.

The younger ranchers are like untamed stallions – they don't like to be fenced in and use up all of their energy trying to impress an entire herd rather than a single mare.

The older ranchers are more like a tired cow dog – rather than go after the cows, they will just wait for one to walk by and nip at her heels to get her attention, but then decide it's too much trouble to pursue her.

Fortunately there are several things a gal can do to hog-tie, connive and cajole a rancher of any age into matrimony. It's not that ranchers don't want to get married — they do — they just don't know it yet and it's up to us women to bring it to their attention.

One of the most direct ways to get a rancher to marry you is to use his own ranching equipment against him. The most difficult part of this strategy is getting him into the cattle chute. Fortunately every rancher has a hotshot cattle prod or two lying around. First give him a good charge to the seat of his pants to get his attention. To begin with he will think you are just joking around like he was all of those times he poked you in the fanny with the hot shot. (One side benefit to using this technique is revenge!)

Once you have his attention, call your mother (who you had the foresight to hide in the barn earlier) to help. There are very few forces on earth more powerful than a mother and daughter with hot shots in their hands and marriage on their minds.

After you have maneuvered him into the chute and secured him in the head catch, grab your cell phone. Every woman trying to land a rancher husband should have her pastor on speed dial and should give him a hefty deposit to get him at a moment's notice. Once your pastor is in the air on the jet you reserved, he will be able to parachute down directly in front of the chute in a matter of minutes.

As the pastor proceeds with the recitation of the wedding vows, it is absolutely imperative that you have your mother stand in front of the chute with the hot shot ready to give your rancher a "gentle" prod as needed. For the really marriage shy rancher, you may need your mother to hang around for a few years afterward to remind him of his sacred commitment to you.

If you prefer a more traditional church wedding you can use his own dogs against him, if you start two weeks prior and sneak them a little prime rib every day. This will take some planning as it will require you to learn the whistle and word commands needed to get the dogs to herd your rancher to the church. Once again, as with the hotshot method, the success of this plan requires that you have your mother ready and waiting to help.

If you are worried he won't follow through, once the dogs have herded him to the altar, in spite of your mother's best efforts, the night before the husband drive, invite your rancher over to your parent's home. Once there, have your Dad and older brother spend the evening cleaning their 12-gauge shotguns and state that they are "getting things ready in case of a family emergency." He won't have any idea of what they are talking about at the time, but it will become quite clear as he is herded to the altar.

And if all else fails, sneak up behind your intended rancher to be with a calf hook. Hook it around his ankle, stretching his leg behind him until he falls to the ground. Then, jump on his back and sit astride him and hold him down for a few minutes while you shove a couple of chocolate covered cherries into his mouth. Sure, he will kick and scream at first, but then when he tires of the struggle he will realize how useful you could be at doctoring calves and will pop the question: "Will you marry me and be my ranch hand?" Well, I'll admit, "being" his hand rather than "taking" his hand in marriage isn't ideal, but once you get that ring on his finger you can work out those minor details by making up the couch for him to sleep on and giving his dinner to the afore mentioned dogs.

I must admit, although these tactics are proven to work, I didn't have to resort to any of them to nab my rancher. My rancher was middle aged, between the young stallion and the tired dog, which is an easier age to capture. Parents of middle-aged ranchers begin to worry that their sons won't ever settle down and start a family. So when his Dad found out we were dating he offered me three cows and a pig to marry his son providing I promise to keep him home on the ranch and curb his spending. And it has worked out really well — I had always wanted a pig...just teasing honey!

O.K., this time when the rancher tries to get us through the gate, you fake left Larry, and the rest of us will scatter.

Sorting It Out

Sorting cattle seems to be an ongoing chore for ranchers. It's kind of like doing dishes; once you think you're done, they somehow get messed up again.

There's always the adventurous (we have other names for this type of cattle, but adventurous will do for now) critter that is constantly getting mixed into a herd where it doesn't belong and no amount of coaxing, herding or cussing will make it come out. So more often than not, you have to bring in the entire herd just to sort out one.

And, several times during the year the bulls have to be sorted from the cows, the cows have to be sorted from the calves, the steers have to be sorted from the heifers, the heifers that you want to keep have to be sorted from the heifers that you want to sell and of course the sick have to be sorted from the healthy.

For those of you who are unfamiliar with how the sorting process works, it always involves gates, and there are usually about five different green gates that ranching husbands always refer to individually as "the green gate," no matter which one he's talking about.

Here's a typical scenario: All of the cows and calves are herded from the pastures into a large holding pen near the corrals, which is a major task in itself. Most of the cows have been into the corrals and chutes before and it's almost as hard to get them to enter the holding pen as it is to get a ranching husband to go to the doctor.

Most of you ranch wives have probably experienced this — your husband will run around and around the car avoiding the open door when you try to coax him into going to the doctor, and he will keep bypassing it until you tactically throw a power tool into the seat. Cows are the same way. They will run around and around the pasture bypassing the gate until you throw some alfalfa into the pen or until you make them think they have a good chance of kicking you as they run through the gate.

Anyway, once the cows and calves are in the pen and you've spent another two hours chasing down the lone steer calf that decided to impress his friends by running to the far back corner of the field, you are ready to get started.

Usually it's set up to where the husband is at the beginning of the corral alleyway herding the cattle toward the wife who is in charge of opening the correct gate, each one opening into a pen that will hold either the cows, the heifers, the steers, or a sick critter, depending on how you decide to sort.

Ideally, "small" groups of cows and calves will be let into the system of corrals at one time to make the sorting easier. But what usually happens, since the cows are agitated at being in the corrals anyway, they are anxious to get out and will all try to come into the corrals at once.

So as the husband officially announces, "Let the sorting begin," and opens the gate, the cows and calves come running into the corrals and down the alleyway toward the wife, similar to the running of the bulls in Pamplona, Spain.

Of course the husband gave the wife explicit instructions before the festivities began of which gates to open and when. So, as the cattle come galloping toward her, the husband, trying to sort them as they run in the gate, yells, "Cow, open the green gate; steer, open the green gate; sick one open the other green gate." In a flurry of flying green gates the wife runs from side to side of the alley letting the appropriate cattle into their respective pens.

Ten minutes and 100 brazen cows later, as the wife stands in the vacant alleyway panting and out of breath, the husband walks up to examine her work. He looks carefully in each of the pens, each containing a mixture of cows and calves, and declares, "Alright, good job! Now open all of the green gates, let them out and we'll see if we can get it right next time."

"Okay," says the wife. "But, could you call them something besides green gates. It gets a little confusing because, well...I don't know... maybe it's because they're all green!"

Sensing he may be on the verge of losing his free help as well as the prospect of having to eat dinner out, he readily complies and says he will try to better identify which gate he is referring to.

This time as the cattle come running down the alleyway toward the wife again, he yells, "Steer, open the green gate that's bent— no, not that gate – the other bent gate, no, the other green gate that's bent on the end, not in the middle..."

Exasperated, the wife yells, "Oh yeah, I see. You mean the other bent green one. They're all green and they're all bent for crying out loud!"

Not knowing what else to do he yells, "Lunch time, honey. How about going back to the house and fixing us something."

To which the wife responds, "Sure, just make sure you don't use the brown door to come into the house. Oh, I forgot, all of the doors are brown, too bad…"

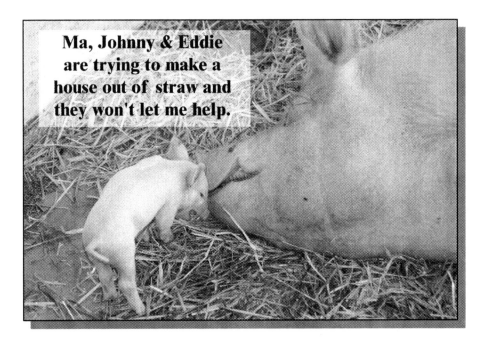

Ma, Johnny & Eddie are trying to make a house out of straw and they won't let me help.

Watching the Blue Channel

My husband and I finally took the plunge. After years of adjusting rabbit ears, turning the television in different directions, and trying to decipher blurry scenes and mumbling actors, we decided to get satellite TV. And it opened up a whole new experience for us – the blue channel.

The blue channel shows everything that is on, has been on, and is going to be on, with areas to click the remote to find out more about each program. So now instead of spending all of our time fiddling to get a better reception, we spend all of our time in that vast blue area clicking through the channel descriptions trying to decide what to watch.

Going from 5 channels to 150 for a rancher is like going from the corner grocery store to a Wal-mart super store — by the time you find where your favorite chocolate chip cookies should be, they don't make them any more. We found a couple of weekly shows that we wanted to watch and by the time we sorted through the list and found them, we tuned in just in time to see the ending credits.

Now, every night after dinner instead of my husband saying, "Well, should we go watch Everybody Loves Raymond?" it's " Should we go watch the blue channel?"

But, with the new satellite we have finally discovered the reality shows that everyone is talking about. We tried watching a few like "America's Top Model," "Nanny 911," "The Biggest Looser," "Big Brother," "The Bachelor," "Survivor," and "American Idol," but quickly realized that most of them have the same ending – someone gets upset and cries. They may be different sexes, different sizes and in different places, but someone always cries in the end. And, watching someone cry is really not very entertaining, as my husband will attest. "Shoot," he says to me, "If I want to see someone cry, I'll just give you a little constructive criticism while we're branding calves."

We did decide however, there are some "reality" shows that we would like to see on TV. One we thought of is our version of Donald Trump's "The Apprentice," called "The Hired Hand." In this show the hired hands arrive in the spring to do all the fieldwork for free to experience the "reality" of ranching. Once the season is over, no one gets fired and no one cries. If fact, they are all asked to come back the next year to work again. And since we would like to help, the network can use our ranch to film it. It would be a tremendous sacrifice on our part to let someone do all the work while we watch, but it would be worth it to help provide quality family entertainment.

A ranch would also be a great setting for a show like "Fear Factor." Instead of seeing how long they can hold their breath while stuffing cockroaches up their nose, and sticking their heads in a vat of slime, they could muck stalls with their bare hands and milk a cow with a really poopie tail. For the courageous daredevil stunts performed on that show participants could see if they could administer a vaccine to a newborn calf with the mother standing near by. Hey, that might tie right in with another popular reality show — "Survivor."

"Dancing with the Stars" and "Skating With Celebrities," I admit are actually pretty entertaining for reality shows. But, wouldn't you rather see Stars "Wrestling With the Hogs," and Celebrities "Skating With Ranchers on an Icy Field While Carrying a Wet Calf?"

"Trading Spouses" has possibilities for the ranch wife. The trade could happen during branding time. The ranch wife would get to go to the city and spend a few days lounging in spas and shopping while the ranch husband would have to see how well the city wife handled the afore mentioned "constructive criticism."

Unfortunately, the networks haven't gotten back to us on the possibility of airing our versions of reality TV shows yet, but we did finally search the blue channel long enough to find a few of our favorites. We are currently watching shows on five of the 150 channels that we have — the same five that we had before we installed the satellite.

Cowlicks — the original spiked hairdo.

Who? Who? Who?

Ranchers have all kinds of critters on their property. There's the domestic kind – the cows, dogs, cats, pigs, and horses. Then, there's the wild kind, which includes raccoons, porcupines and weasels. And, then there's the unwanted kind like coyotes, gophers and cougars. But we have recently come across a new category — the neat to see, fun to have around, but the too talkative kind.

We first noticed the latter kind of critter the other morning at breakfast. Usually breakfast consists of both of us eating, me talking and my husband, Mike, reading the newspaper. I was talking away about some incident that happened in town and for once I thought he was paying attention to what I was saying, because he asked a question.

About two sentences into my story he said, "Who?" which is a big change from his usual grunt that he gives me when I tell a story.

43

So, I politely told him the person's name again and he then responded with his usual grunt, but I thought at least that was some progress. So I continued with my story and got a little further along when he said, "Who?" again.

"I told you who," I said.

"What?" said Mike.

"Who, I told you who; in fact, I told you who twice," I said. "Now you want to know what?"

"What?" said Mike again a little perplexed.

"O.K.," I said starting to get a little exasperated, and started all over with my story. Mike kind of shook his head and went back to reading the paper.

Just as I was about to get to the point of my story he did it again – he said, "Who?"

"How many times do I have to tell you who?" I asked.

"I don't know. I was beginning to wonder the same thing, you already told me who three times," he said.

"What?" I said.

"I think you told me what about half a dozen times," he said. "In fact, it's starting to get a little annoying."

Just then, while we were both facing each other, another rarity at breakfast, I head it again, "Who?" This time I knew it wasn't Mike because his lips didn't move and needless to say his ventriloquism sounds like a squeaky wheel stuck in the mud.

"Did you hear that?" I said.

"Oh that," answered Mike, "look out the kitchen window. It's a great horned owl, he's been hanging around all morning."

Once we finally settled who was saying, "who," I forgot who and what I was talking about and breakfast was over anyway. But the owl has been hanging around for over a week now and continues to ask us who every morning, every evening and all night long.

44

In fact, the other night he kept it up so long I finally got up, opened the window, and yelled, "Don't you ever want to know anything else like what, where or why?"

Fortunately, Mike can sleep with the owl hooting, but he says my yelling is a little harder to ignore... I've since decided I might try yelling while we are eating breakfast and see if that's a little harder to ignore too....

It never hurts to have all of your geese in a row too.

The Unsuspecting
City Slicker

Even after 17 years of living on the ranch, I have always been our family's "city slicker." That's why I'm always tickled when I get an opportunity to explain things to other citified folks — like my brother, Tom, for instance.

He lives in the big city area of Portland, Ore., and recently came for a visit. It just so happens that he was here right around the time we normally work our cows and calves. Well, I have to be honest, that's not completely true. We found out he was coming and decided to take advantage of the situation. After all, my mom can't do everything!

We were careful not to tell him of our plans until he arrived and got settled in.

"Oh, by the way," I said casually. "You will need to get up at 5 a.m. tomorrow to help with the cattle." I learned a long time ago not to phrase the job of working cattle into a question such as "Would you like to help us work cattle tomorrow?" That would give unsuspecting relatives the idea that they could say "no" — something we really want to avoid.

"What exactly does it mean 'to help with the cattle'?" he asked.

"Oh, the usual," I said. "You know, giving shots, wormer, applying stuff for lice, etc… nothing too difficult," I assured him.

He shot a puzzled look at Mom who has learned over the years that giving too much information and scaring away any potential help means more work for her. "What does she mean etc.?" he asked.

Mom just shrugged her shoulders and said, "Isn't dinner about ready?"

We managed to keep him occupied the rest of the evening so he would have little time to think about the events that would take place the next day. And at 5 a.m. the next morning he came bouncing down the stairs ready to go — wearing his crisp white, L.L. Bean polo shirt and brand new white sneakers.

I quickly assessed the situation and asked, "Is there any reason that your white shirt and shoes would need to remain white?"

"What do you mean?" he said.

Rummaging through the closet I found an old flannel shirt and a pair of rubber boots and handed them to him. Not wanting to call attention to his obvious ranch fashion faux pas, I said, "I think you would be happier dressed like the rest of us."

He surveyed the motley looking crew, consisting of my mom, my husband and myself, standing before him wearing yellow-stained baggy jeans and overalls, flannel shirts, and rubber boots caked with last year's cow poop, topped off with equally blemished Bud Light baseball hats.

I'm sure at that point he must have concluded that it had been a tough year for us financially, as he graciously conceded without another comment, and put on the attire I handed him.

"One more thing," I said as we walked out the door. I handed Tom a pair of gloves, "You'll need these."

"Nah, that's O.K.," he said. "I don't need any gloves."

"Suit yourself," I said, and stuffed them in my pocket.

We got the cows and calves sorted without too much effort — that is after the mandatory time it takes to allow a newcomer to play "Rawhide" when they first get a whip into their hands.

My husband lined us out on our duties, my mom and brother would help him at the calf table, closing the head and tail gates, administering shots, and etc., while I pushed the calves up the chute.

It took a couple of calves to get any kind of a routine down. I pushed the first calf up to the table and told my brother to open the tailgate so I could let it in. He looked around for a minute and finally said, "Where's the button?"

Once he got over the surprise that there was no button and he had to manually grab the gate and pull it open, he quickly got the hang of it. The first few calves went through pretty smooth and I could see my brother was starting to enjoy himself…that is until the fourth calf. The fourth calf was bigger than most, was stubborn, and had a bad case of diarrhea to boot. I got the calf up to the table, but he wouldn't go any further. The more I pushed on him the more he locked his front legs and the more his rear end went up in the air along with the afore mentioned diarrhea.

So my husband said, "Tom, grab that calf by the tail and give it a little twist while Deb pushes on him to get him to move."

Did I mention this calf had really bad diarrhea? Tom took one look at the calf's tail and looked at me in complete disgust.

"That would be the reason for the gloves," I said, as I pulled them out of my pocket and handed them to him. He put on the gloves and gingerly grabbed the calf's tail between his thumb and forefinger, and while holding his breath gave it a gentle twist. About that time I raised myself up on the sides of the chute and shoved him the rest of the way with both of my feet.

After a few more calves he got the hang of it and was grabbing and twisting tails and wrangling calves like he had been doing it forever. He finally realized, like the rest of us, that calf poop was just part of the job and something you had to put up with. He even quit wrinkling up his nose every time one with diarrhea came through. He did find out the hard way though that you have to be mindful of taking your gloves off before you scratch your nose.

When he helped me push cows through the chute he also quickly learned the reason for the rubber boots, and stopped his futile attempts of trying to step around the cow pies, and learned to slide through them like the rest of us.

Being the good sport that he is, it wasn't until the end of the day that we realized the boots we had given him to wear were about a size too small. We all thought he was really getting into the whole ranching thing and was walking like a bow-legged cowboy on purpose — until he took off his boots and had to manually flatten out his curled toes.

I asked him later what he thought about the whole ranching thing and he said it's just like any other business, "The more money you make the more 'crap' you have to put up with."

Now that he's a "seasoned" rancher, next year he says he's bringing his city slicker wife, Belinda. I heard him call her on the phone, "Nah, you'll love visiting here next spring. Just make sure you bring those fancy new leather Italian shoes, you know, the ones with the open toes that you paid $200 for, you'll have some good opportunities here to wear them…Yeah, and don't let me forget to throw in my hip waders."

Diamonds really can be a girl's best friend.

Cat on a Hot Tin Roof

I've always been more of a dog person myself, but cats do have their place on a ranch and we always have a few wild cats in the barn to help keep the rodent population down.

We feed the cats to keep them around, but we hardly ever see them; however, we have had several opportunities to hear them. For some reason the cats have chosen the area below our bedroom window to settle their differences of opinion. Likewise, this is also where they like to have their romantic interludes. Both of these activities are accompanied by unearthly high-pitched squealing sounds, and for some reason are only performed in the middle of the night. Two a.m. seems to be a popular time for these rituals.

But, like I said, cats do have their place on a ranch, unfortunately they don't always know where their place is. One morning we discovered a wild cat on the metal roof of a lean-to near our cattle loading chutes down a hill about 200 yards from the house. This ordinarily wouldn't be cause for concern, but we noticed after a few days that this cat was still on that roof and the temperatures were in the 90s.

"I wonder why that cat keeps sitting up there on that hot tin roof?" I asked my husband, Mike, one morning. "Maybe he can't get down."

Sensing that this situation could easily turn into a chore for him he quickly replied, "Don't worry. When he gets hungry enough he'll figure out a way to get down — after all, he's not stupid."

As it turns out though, this cat was apparently just that — stupid. The next morning I was at home sick with the flu so had ample opportunity to see this cat from our bedroom window and he was still on the roof.

I got out the binoculars and took a closer look at this feral feline and told my husband that I didn't think this poor animal could last any longer on the roof without food and water.

"He'll get down when he wants to," he assured me. But about every hour, since I had to get out of bed anyway with those annoying symptoms that accompany the flu, I would look out the window and give my husband, who was trying to get some work done in the office, updates on the cat's lack of progress.

"He's still just sitting there, starving to death," I would say. "Can you image how hot it must be up there, especially if you were dehydrated from going four days without water?"

After two or three of these updates I looked out the window and saw Mike heading down the hill from our house to the lean-to. I got out my binoculars and saw that he had a bowl of cat food and a couple of 2x4s. He placed the 2x4s across the loading chute onto the roof to form a ramp for the cat and then placed the food at the bottom of the ramp to lure it down from the roof.

As I sat and watched with the binoculars, after my husband had returned to the house to resume his work, I continued the updates. "The cat hasn't seen the food yet. Did you give him some water too? Maybe you need to put some water on the roof so he will have the strength to try and climb down the ramp."

I listened… no response came from the downstairs office. But, as I watched out the window, I saw Mike once again walking down the hill, this time with a bowl of water. He climbed up the chute and placed the water on the edge of the roof.

When he got back into the house I continued the play-by-play updates. "He's looking at the bowl. He's walking toward the water and yes, he's drinking it!"

A few minutes later the cat walked down the ramp and began eating the food that Mike had placed there. "He's eating the food," I yelled. Then, as I watched, the cat did a really stupid thing further negating Mike's previous remark about his possible intelligence. He walked back, halfway up the ramp, and turned and climbed up a board and ended up on a four-foot long 2x4 braced across the top of the chute and once again became stranded.

"Now he's stuck on top of the chute," I called to Mike. "He's just walking back and forth on a board and can't get down."

Mike, now becoming slightly irritated at the situation said, "If he can get up there on his own he can get down on his own! I'm trying to get some work done!"

For once I decided to give Mike the benefit of the doubt and concluded that maybe he was right. If the cat was smart enough to crawl down and get the food, maybe he could get down after all.

So, I went back to bed and fell asleep for a little while and once again was wakened by the flu symptoms. This time I looked out the window and a magpie had landed right in front of the cat and the cat was just sitting there looking at him.

Not wanting Mike to miss any of the action, I reported this new development to him. "The cat's not even trying to chase the bird away," I said. "Why would a bird get that close to a cat… wait a minute…the bird is pecking the cat on the head. The cat is just sitting there taking it, if he could get down why doesn't he get away from the bird? That cat must be in pretty bad shape to take a beating from a bird...did you hear me? The bird is pecking his head..."

Just about that time I realized Mike was no longer listening to my reports, in fact he was no longer in the house. He was walking down the hill with a ladder. As I continued to peer through my binoculars I saw him position the ladder beneath the chute and then go to the nearby barn. Moments later he came out of the barn with thick welding gloves on that reached to his elbows.

As I watch the events unfold, Mike climbed the ladder and snatched up the cat in his gloved hands. As I soon found out, the "poor, dehydrated, half-starved" cat actually had a lot more energy left in him than anyone would have suspected. The scene looked similar to a game of "Hot Potato" as Mike tried to hang onto the twisting, hissing ball of fur. All of this commotion almost knocked Mike off his ladder, but the cat finally managed to wiggle out of his grasp and hit the ground running.

Satisfied that the cat was now out of danger, I went back to bed and slept off the flu the rest of the day.

The next morning I felt much better and while we were at the table eating breakfast I looked out the window and exclaimed, "The yellow cat's back on the tin roof again!"

As I jumped up to grab the binoculars I briefly caught a glimpse of Mike and could have sworn I saw visions of little .22 rifles dancing in his eyes.

"On second thought," I said, "I'm sure he's not stupid... he should be able to find his own way down when he gets hungry enough — don't you think?"

Who's the
Sheep Dip Here?

After I got over my milk cow and chicken phases, I decided sheep would be my next adventure. I thought if Mary could have a little lamb that followed her, by golly so could I. I soon found out that although lambs may be willing to follow you around, ewes don't seem to want you around – this is evidenced by their eagerness to shove you out of the way. Whoever decided that sheep were so docile and serene that they could be used to induce sleep, apparently hasn't ever been head butted in the hip by one.

We purchased 16 ewes and I had visions of getting to know each one of them so well that I could tell them apart and give them individual names like "Sweet Pea" and "Honey." Turns out I named them collectively as a flock — "Sheep Dips," a term, which was usually preceded by a few expletives.

The first time I went out in the field to gather the ewes and take them to a new pasture, I took my sheepherder's staff. I didn't know at the time why I needed a staff, but I'd seen pictures of sheepherders and they all seemed to have one.

This is when I discovered that they really don't follow you. I could have stood out there until their wool grew so long it hit the ground and they still wouldn't have made any effort to come in my direction. So, I figured they must be like cattle; I'll just herd them through the gate. The sheep quickly gathered in a tight little group and proceeded to run almost as one. I thought, wow, this will be a lot easier than cattle; there are no stragglers to go back for.

The only problem was that tight little mass of wool and beady eyes wouldn't run in the direction I wanted them to. As it so happens, the field they were in had a road going through it, which acted as a turn around for equipment making a loop around the field. They got on this road and ran around it like runners at a track and field event. Every time I would get in front of them and try to push them back the other way toward the gate, they would just run around the track in the opposite direction.

After two hours I finally figured out what that staff was for. I caught a couple of the ewes around the hind foot with the crooked end and wrestled them through the gate, thinking the others might follow if they see one in the other field. But they would squirt back out between my legs before I could get the gate closed and rejoin the other sheep still running the 1/4-mile.

I finally sat down exhausted and realized that the sheep might not be the only dips in the field because I had continued to run around the track after them for the better part of the morning before finally going to get help. With my husband's assistance, we were finally able to herd the sheep through the gate, but even with both of us, it wasn't easy.

Shortly after this incident we decided what we really needed was a good sheep-herding dog. So, for 16 ewes, that get moved about once every three weeks, we went out and bought a $1,500 dog. Again, the question of the rightful owner of the title "Sheep Dips" comes to mind…

58

Don't get me wrong, the dog performed beautifully. After I learned a few of the commands she went out and moved the sheep through the same gate that took me half a day to get them through, in 15 minutes. But, with only that to do once every few weeks, she became bored and took it upon herself to move them whenever she felt like it. Only problem is she couldn't figure out how to open the gate and ended up much like me, running them in circles around the track.

I finally got to where we went out and moved the sheep somewhere every day, just so she would have something to do. But, she was a hard worker and that still wasn't enough. She eventually decided to start herding the cattle, horses, pigs, chickens, and barn cats by herself. When we really realized we were in trouble though is when she started trying to herd our friends and relatives out to their cars. Unfortunately, our attempts at getting her to herd salesmen away from the house were unsuccessful — if she would have done that we might have kept her around a little longer. But, we realized she needed to be on a ranch with more than 16 ewes or we would have to keep her in a kennel, which seemed unfair because all she wanted to do was work, so we sold her.

I did, however, manage to keep the sheep until they lambed that first year. I really didn't know anything about sheep and was so surprised one evening when the first ewe to lamb had twins. I came running back to the house jumping up and down, "We've got twins, we've got twins!"

About an hour later I came running back into the house announcing to anyone who would listen, "We've got triplets! Can you believe it? There are three of the little buggers!"

A few days into lambing and after several more times of me running around excitedly announcing the news of multiple births, someone finally told me that almost all ewes have twins and triplets.

An experienced sheep rancher also told me that if I wanted the sheep to follow me around, all I had to do was grain them. Sure enough, as soon as they figured out what I had in the bucket, every day they ran up to greet me at the feed trough. It even got to where I could pet and scratch them while they ate, although it was more like I was an annoying fly on

59

their backside that they couldn't reach so they tolerated me. But like little Mary in the nursery rhyme, everywhere I went the sheep finally did follow me.

All of this makes me wonder though...did Mary's little lamb really follow her to school one day or did she bribe it with a bucket of grain?

Eat More Beef

Please...

Zucchini — The Duct Tape of Vegetables

The 1978 movie thriller, "Attack of the Killer Tomatoes," depicted people running and screaming as giant tomatoes chased them slinging deadly tomato juice, but the fleshy red fruit had nothing over zucchini. The annual zucchini invasion is almost upon us and although not as deadly as the killer tomato, the vegetable has the ability to reproduce itself faster than a sci-fi alien army, and can grow so large you could hollow it out to make a four-man canoe.

If someone hadn't somewhere along the way discovered that zucchini was edible, I'm sure it would be on the County's noxious weeds list today, requiring mandatory control right up there with Tansy Ragwort and Dalmation Toadflax. Pesticide manufactures would be spending millions of dollars developing chemicals like "Zucchini Be Gone," "Squash Terminator," and "Zap A Zuch."

But, since we can eat it, I, along with many others, actually plant, water, and weed it every year in anticipation of that first batch of fried zucchini and that mouth-watering loaf of zucchini bread. The only problem is over the long winter months we have a tendency to forget the 500 batches of fried zucchini and the 247 loaves of zucchini bread we had to continually force ourselves to choke down last summer in order to keep up with prolific vegetable.

Fortunately over the years, zucchini connoisseurs have developed 110,532,451 recipes for the succulent squash — everything from, fricasseed and frapped zucchini to stuffed, marinated, smashed, broiled, barbecued, pickled, and packed. But, when you get to the point where you just can't stomach it any more and your garden is still abounding with the green schlop on a vine, there are many other things you can do with them. If you use your imagination, Zucchini can be the "duct tape" of vegetables.

For instance, when you take the cork out of a bottle of fine wine by chewing it up into little pieces with a corkscrew (cork screws never work as they were intended) you can replace the cork with a chunk of zucchini. I'm sure Martha Stewart would approve of this one. Likewise, why waste money on expensive repair jobs when holes in the walls, tractor radiators, and household appliances can all be fixed with a simple "zuch plug" — it's a good thing!

To rid yourself of massive quantities of zucchini, secretly teach your kids to have sword fights with the longer ones and tell them to engage in this activity at will. The only catch is when they have broken and beaten the zucchini down to a few smashed pieces at your mother's house, you have to act indignant that they would waste good food like this... and then make it up to them later.

If you have a dog that likes to have objects thrown for them to retrieve, but they never actually bring them back, try tossing out a few zucchini Frisbees. The only drawback is that you may end up with chunks of chewed up squash all over your yard, but, similar to the sword fighting, you can blame it on the dog, and later, when no one is looking, give the dog a T-bone.

Since your friends and neighbors are onto you from previous years, and won't open the door or answer the phone when you call, you have to think of other ways to distribute your bounty like packing zucchini around with you in your purse. When someone gives you a service such as the gas station attendant, beautician, or store clerk, you can reach into your purse and tell them that you would like to give them a little something extra for their time and trouble. As they eagerly wait for their cash award, you can whip out a zucchini and they will be too embarrassed to refuse it.

One of the most obvious is to hold drive by vegetable flingings. Load up the truck with zucchini and kids and have the youngsters hurl them onto doorsteps like a hot off the press newspaper. Most people won't notice the difference until you're long gone and it's too late to give it back. And, if you are in the middle of an election, you can even sell advertising space on the zucchinis like "Squash Taxes, Vote For Smith," making this venture more profitable than most. Just make sure you don't smack anyone on the head with a out-of-control zucchini or you'll be looking at possibly getting squashed yourself or worse yet facing a "intent to do harm with a dangerous vegetable" charge.

When you get down to the point that all of the zucchini you have left are too large to do anything else with you can travel around the country entering your fine specimens in the County Fairs. They won't know that your entries are the result of neglecting your zucchini patch, and will think that you purposely grew them the size of a small whale to beat out the competition. However, upon leaving your giant vegetables, you must not return to get your ribbons when the zucchini judging is over, because they will think you have come to pick up your trophy squash and you will inevitably get stuck with it again.

There are a few other cautionary measures that you can take to avoid the phenomena known as the "zucchini boomerang effect" where you receive more of them back than you gave away. During zucchini season:

• Never leave your car windows rolled down. It's too tempting to a passerby toting a sack full of zucchini;

• Don't let your kids or your husband leave the house. They're fair game to others trying to rid themselves of the squash;

• Never go to a potluck because everyone will bring zucchini dishes;

• Don't let the neighbors in if they are carrying anything that could be used to disguise zucchini in and don't be afraid to frisk them if necessary. In the heat of the squash season, people have been know to stuff a zucchini or two up their pant legs and under their arms pits.

• And finally, when you encounter a known zucchini donor, shove a sack of zucchini in their hands before they have a chance to speak, to avoid being given one yourself.

By taking a few simple precautions you'll survive the zucchini season, and don't worry, zucchini won't hurt you like the killer tomatoes; it will only make you unpopular with your family and friends for a while.

Please Mom, everyone else gets to go to the barn dance. Betsy's Mom is even letting her borrow her ear tags.

Ranchers Are All about Style

I have been keeping an eye on the fashion trends these days and I've concluded that ranchers are inherently some of the trendiest dressers around, particularly when it comes to jeans.

Fashion conscious individuals are paying big bucks to get jeans that are what they call "distressed." I'm sure they must have machines that do this sort of thing in the fashion industry that rip them in strategic places, pull threads up from the material, and make permanent creases. But ranchers have all of these benefits without paying the extra cost.

The thing is, almost all rancher's jeans are distressed – climb over a couple of barbed wire fences, hook them on a few exposed nails, and for permanent creases sit in a tractor seat for three days straight and you've got authentic "distressed" jeans.

Many other jean styles were actually developed by ranchers.

"Wide leg" jeans were invented when cow dogs continually grabbed a hold of a rancher's pant legs and tugged on them while they were walking to the barn. This also contributed to the "distressed" and "frayed' looks, and was the precursor to "cutoff" shorts.

"Elastic waist" jeans were made out of necessity as the rancher became more and more fond of pork, and it became impolite to undo your top button and fly at the dinner table.

The popular "push up" jeans, which lift your derriere, have been around for quite some time and began when ranchers started using baling twine to hike up their jeans.

"Boot cut" was developed by ranchers who liked to put on their boots and spurs before their jeans. With the invention of these jeans ranchers felt they had a justification for sleeping with their boots on to speed up the dressing process in the morning, but this style never went over well with rancher's wives.

One of the most popular current styles, "baggy" jeans, was initially invented by ranchers with large families, who being cost conscious, passed jeans down from the older children to the younger as they outgrew them. Unlike city folks, though, tripping over the bottoms got in the way of chasing cattle and having the crotches hang down to their knees became a problem when wearing hip high irrigation boots. So, instead, they reversed the order and began "handing up" jeans from the younger to the older children and invented the "hipster" and "tight leg" jeans as well as "stretch" jeans.

"Straight leg" jeans were actually the result of ranchers wearing their jeans for three weeks straight without washing them and they discovered their jeans would no longer bend at the knees. It was kind of fun at first, but as with the "baggy" style, there were problems. Cows were not easily intimidated by the comic look of a family of ranchers chasing them with inflexible knees, and laughing cows are not easily herded. Horses were also not fond of this style as ranchers had to be hoisted above the horse by a pulley system to get seated in the saddle.

However, there are some styles of jeans that ranchers only wear when doing specific jobs. The popular "low rise" jeans are only worn while working on the plumbing or doing odd jobs around the house that require a lot of squatting and bending over.

Manufacturers claim that jeans come in several different colors, but upon close observation, it appears they are just in different stages of wearing out. For instance "dark denim" jeans are jeans that have only been washed once or twice. "Medium light" jeans have been washed and worn about 30 times and "light denim" jeans have definitely seen better days.

Ranchers, however, were the first to invent the "white wash" color, which are actually jeans that have been worn while cleaning out the chicken coop. And for the "antique" or "vintage" color, cow poop provides a nice yellowish worn look to jeans that stays in the material even after numerous washings.

"Bleached" jeans are a spin off from the "antique" styles that originated with rancher's wives when they tried to get the cow poop out, and "stonewash" jeans are pretty much out of vogue since the invention of the washing machine.

Ranchers have come up with a few styles and colors that haven't reached the fashion industry yet – "grass stained" jeans, "dog slobber" jeans, "pig slop" jeans, "broken fly" jeans, "busted bottom" jeans, "grease tint" jeans, and jeans with various outdoor odors — "scratch and sniff" jeans.

I suspect it's only a matter of time before the rest of the population catches on to these styles as they have the others. It's just a shame that ranchers don't receive any monetary compensation for their worthwhile contributions to the fashion industry.

Honest!
The vet
said I
should
have
banana
cream
pie
every
day!

Food to Motivate, Exercise to Compensate

I read a complimentary copy of a health magazine I received in the mail a few days ago and it said to stay healthy, don't eat anything that isn't food. I thought great — I can do that — I don't like eating dirt and paper anyway.

As I continued to read, I made some startling discoveries — did you know that potato chips aren't a food? According to this magazine anything that has preservatives, hydrogenated oils and processed flour or sugar in it isn't a food. What the heck does that leave — cod liver oil and brussle sprouts?

Although this information was interesting, I think I would rather go with the Muppet character, Miss Piggy's, advice, who said, "Never eat more than you can lift." I'm used to moving around 90 pound bales of hay so I think I'm good!

Trying to figure out how to eat healthy is really difficult, especially when food comes in handy for so many things including motivation. I've discovered, like the proverbial carrot dangling in front of the horse's nose, I too, will move forward with the proper incentive.

I have a good friend, and fellow writer, Sherrie, who emailed and asked me not too long ago if I had any secrets to making myself sit down at the computer and write when I'd rather be outside playing.

"Sure," I wrote back to her, "strawberry shortcake."

If I make myself a big bowl of cake with strawberries and whipped topping or ice cream, I can pace myself better. I sit it in front of my keyboard and for every bite I take, I need to write four more sentences before I can have another bite.

She tried this technique and reported success even on a nice sunny day when she would rather be outside!

The only problem with eating to write is that you have to get in enough exercise to compensate for the added calories, especially if you are writing a 10-page project. So, periodically throughout the day as we are writing, we email each other and offer encouragement like this exchange we had recently:

"Have you gotten any exercise yet?" I asked.

"I tried kickboxing and liked it until I got to the kickboxing part!" she said. "The warm-ups were wonderful. I even played music I was a little familiar with, but I can't afford to replace all of the lamps and coffee tables that fall victim to my uncontrolled kicks and jabs. Besides, the neighbors might think there is a big fight going on with all the noise, and call the police. Did you spend some time on your elliptical machine or did you get 'derailed'?"

"I'm going to go jump on my elliptical right now," I responded "so I will get back to you in a little while."

"I'm going to go get on mine right now, too," she said, "and if it doesn't buck me off, I'll come back to this computer...hopefully less than what I was!"

An hour later, back at the computers, Sherrie emailed: "How did it go?"

"Well, I did jump on my elliptical," I responded. "Once I managed to get a hold of the bars so they would stop slapping me in the face, it went pretty well I think. I couldn't find anything on T.V. to watch while I was exercising and finally ended up watching an infomercial about the GT Xpress 101. While they were demonstrating the variety of foods it could cook, omelets, tacos, chicken, and desserts, I got hungry and had to stop and get a snack. I got back on the elliptical and somehow ended up on the couch a few minutes later yelling at my husband who was in the other room that we needed to get one of these things.

"It cooks food on both sides in seven minutes and is available for two easy payments of $19.95 each," I yelled.

"We don't need any more kitchen gadgets," he shouted back.

"But it comes with a free spatula," I insisted as he entered the room.

"I thought you were suppose to be exercising," he said looking at me sprawled out on the couch.

"I'm already done," I said as I stomped back to the computer irritated by his insinuation that I might not be living up to my full exercise potential.

"How did it go on your elliptical?" I emailed Sherrie.

"I failed!" Sherrie responded. "I turned on the T.V. and discovered I need to get some movies to have on hand while exercising, there is nothing on. I finally changed the channel to Extreme Makeover and there was a family who couldn't live together because the little girl had to be in HEPA filtered clean air and they lived in a not so sealed mobile home. Well, I started to watch the little girl and all of a sudden was on the couch completely involved and forgot all about exercising...I'll try again later. How's your writing going?"

"Since my last email I got a notice about a sale and decided I better get some shopping done. I went online to jcpenney.com and they have all of these blouses for sale in their outlet store for $9.99-$14.99, and if you order it today — and today only, with your JC Penney card — you get another 15 percent off! Some of the blouses are only $8.50 with that discount!"

"O.K., I'm online at JC Penney and I'm getting my credit card out now," she wrote back.

"Oh, while you're there, check out their wicker lawn furniture – it's on sale too," I emailed.

An hour later, "O.K. I'm back," Sherrie writes. "I had to go outside to figure out what lawn furniture I might need."

"Did you get any exercise while you were out there?" I asked.

"Not unless you count turning the sprinkler on," she replied. "However, it did take some effort to move my chair around to follow the sun. I don't have time to exercise now? I really have to finish this article I'm working on. I started out first thing this morning thinking I would get organized so I would come back to a formatted day...then never got past the formatting! I'll have to try my elliptical again tomorrow."

"I think I'm finally done with my column," I replied. "I must be, my bowl of strawberry shortcake is empty."

How Sweet It Is!

Hot Hay Tarps and
Puddin' Head Follies

August is a great time of year for ranchers — the water wars are dying down as the rivers drop, calving season is over, feeding hasn't begun and most of the hay is baled and stacked. About the only thing left is the yearly job of covering the haystacks to prevent damage from the rain.

Now, one would think that putting tarps on a haystack wouldn't be too complicated, especially on a stack of baled hay that forms a nice flat surface on top. But, one has never encountered a Puddin' Head.

Puddin' Head is our part black lab, and Lord only knows what, dog. And, as her name implies, although quite lovable, she's not Lassie material. To put it mildly, if Timmy were to fall down a well on our ranch, she wouldn't go for help, she wouldn't grab a rope, and she wouldn't even bark to attract attention — she would look down the well wagging her tail and slobber all over the poor little fellow. Fortunately for Timmy, he doesn't come around often.

Puddin' Head does have her good points though. She's friendly, she can run fast, she's friendly, she can jump high and... did I already mention that she's friendly? But let's just say helping cover haystacks isn't one of her stronger attributes, although you do have to give her credit for trying.

It didn't help matters either that we picked the hottest day of the year to stand up on top of a haystack, 25 feet closer to the blazing sun, wrestling with 200 pounds of hot plastic tarp. My husband, Mike, and I used the conventional ladder method to get to the top of the stack. Puddin' Head on the other hand, got a run at it, jumped and hit the stack about center and managed to claw the rest of the way to the top deftly hooking her toes on baling twine like an experienced mountain climber.

We hadn't expected Puddin' Head to offer to help, but once she was on top of the stack we couldn't see any safe way to get her down so decided to let her stay.

Mike had already placed the rolled up tarps on top of the haystack with the tractor's grappling hook so all we needed to do was unroll them. Easy right? Not with a Puddin' Head. She thought it was a game and began jumping on the tarp as we were unrolling it and tried to help by pulling it with her teeth. This wouldn't have been quite so bad if it weren't for the fact that holes in a tarp kind of defeat its intended purpose.

After thoroughly getting yelled at by both of us, she finally decided not to help quite so much and we managed to get the tarp unrolled. Unfortunately, the tarp ended up lopsided, hanging longer on one side than the other, and wasn't covering the end of the stack.

So, Mike decided he would climb down and start fastening the tie downs to see if he could straighten it out and that I should stay on top of the hotter than a pizza oven hay stack in case he needed me to do anything. That's when the real fun began.

I waited for Mike's instructions as he unbeknownst to me began pulling on the tarp from the ground. After about five minutes he yelled up and said, "It must be hung up somewhere, it's not budging. Can you see the problem?"

As I said, I didn't even know he was pulling on it and was still waiting for orders.

"You think it might help if I get off the tarp?" I yelled down to him half laughing.

"Hey, there's an idea," he said. "Why don't you try it...NOW!"

So, Puddin' Head and I made our way over to the two-foot wide strip of uncovered hay at one end where the tarp wouldn't reach, and once again began the waiting process in the sweltering heat. We could see bits of tarp tightening around the stack as Mike continued to struggle with it from the ground.

Exasperated, he finally yelled up and said, "It's not working, you are going to have to pull the tarp over the end and down on one side from up there."

If you have never had the privilege of trying to move a hay tarp while incidentally it is also the only place to stand on, it's similar to trying to make the bed while you're still in it. Now image that...and throw a Puddin' Head on top of it to counteract your every move.

Every piece of tarp I grabbed a hold of to pull, Puddin' Head would firmly plant her seat on top of it. A tarp is heavy enough without a dog sitting on it. Add the 101-degree temperature, the uncomfortable feeling of hot plastic against your skin, a man standing at the bottom of the stack yelling orders, and you've got the makings of one cranky rancher's wife.

So, it was time to take charge, well, at least whine a little. "Can I get down now?" I yelled.

"Unless I'm suffering from heat stroke and it looks a whole lot different up there than it does down here, NO," he said. "We need to get this done."

So, once again I began pulling on the tarp, this time on my hands and knees to get more leverage. I had finally managed to convince Puddin' Head that she couldn't sit on the section of tarp I was pulling on, so she dutifully sat next to me. The only problem with this was that now I was down on all fours at her level, she decided that I needed a good face licking while my hands were busy. Every time I let go of the tarp she would quit, every time I grabbed the tarp she would commence to licking again.

I finally had to walk her over to the previously mentioned two-foot wide strip of uncovered hay at the other end of the stack and make her sit. After another good 20 minutes of tugging and sweating I finally managed to pull the hay tarp over the end and even it out the sides.

"Now, can I get down?" I whined again.

"O.K.," he said. "Make sure Puddin' Head comes with you so I can get everything tightened down on the sides."

Puddin' Head? I looked around; she wasn't on the strip of hay. I scanned the tarp; she was nowhere to be seen. Just as I was thinking that she must have decided to get down when no one was looking, I saw a bulge in the tarp. Puddin' had gotten underneath the tarp and had crawled to the middle of the stack.

I lifted up the end of the tarp and called to her. She didn't budge. I began to get worried that maybe she got under the tarp and got so hot she passed out or something so I went to the lifeless lump in the center of the stack and gently prodded her. She responded by trying to playfully bite my fingers through the tarp.

So, I poked her again, the same response, but this time she moved a little. I had to poke her all the way to the end of the stack slowly edging her out like squirting toothpaste from a tube, until she finally popped her head out from under the tarp and was once again standing on the narrow uncovered strip of hay.

Relieved to find out she was O.K. I finally responded to the insistent voice coming from the ground that had been yelling up at us every few minutes, with "Would you two quit playing around and get down here!"

I climbed down the ladder and before I hit the ground, Puddin' Head was at my feet wagging her tail and jumping and biting at my shoes to make me hurry faster. I have no idea how she got down, but I'm beginning to think besides her obvious lineage of black lab, greyhound, cheetah, and border collie that she must have a little monkey in her as well.

Sometimes a nap makes everything better...

We'll Always Have
Our Moose

Most mornings in a rancher's life are pretty predictable — the sun comes up with nature's alarm of squalling cats and fighting dogs, and the escaped-cow-induced heartburn is easily quenched with a 1/2 bottle of Extra Strength Mylanta. But Sunday morning was a little different...

As I was getting out of bed, I happened to glance out the window and saw the whole herd of cows and their calves running full bore toward the back pasture. As I stood there in my usual too early in the morning to function, with only a half a brain engaged stupor, watching and trying to figure out what the cows were up to, they came to a screeching halt. Fortunately, the whole herd had the same idea otherwise there would have been a bovine pile up of hooves over heads and tails over T-bones.

Just when their outstretched front legs almost brought them to a stop, they simultaneously whirled around and commenced their charge like a band of liquored up Vikings, in the direction they had just come from.

I finally woke up enough to yell down the stairs to my husband, Mike, who was sipping his morning cup of slap-me-in-the-face and wake-me-up coffee.

"What's wrong with your cows?"

"Same thing that's always wrong with your cows — they're spoiled," he said. It's funny how when there is a problem cow ownership dramatically changes. Had they been acting any stranger we probably would have disowned them altogether and said, "What's wrong with the neighbor's cows?"

Still upstairs, I could hear Mike shuffle around the kitchen making his way to the window while muttering something about dumb cows, cold coffee and no breakfast in sight.

The cows were still continuing their early morning pasture charges, running back and forth, only now they had tired to the point that they couldn't run in a straight line and were zigzagging all over the field, barely able to miss colliding with each other.

Mike finally got a handle on the situation. "There's a big black mule in the pasture," he exclaimed.

"Where in the world would a mule come from?" I asked. "I don't recall seeing mules at any of the neighbors."

In order to get a better handle on the situation we decided to get a closer view and this started a 10-minute frenzy of ransacking the house for the binoculars. Now, ordinarily the binoculars are sitting on the kitchen table in the way, or laying on the couch for some unsuspecting soul to plop down on before looking at their landing target, or on the desk anchoring down a stack of unpaid bills. But of course, on this morning when we actually needed them, they were nowhere to be found.

Finally, I found them hanging on a hook that we had specifically placed on the wall several years ago to hang them on.

"How in the world did they get there?" I asked.

"I don't know," said Mike a little exasperated. "We need to quit making designated places to put things. It messes us up."

Fortunately, the "black mule" was still standing there watching the cattle frenzy. Mike took one look through the binoculars and said, "It's a moose!"

"Yeah right," I quipped. "Did you put a little something extra in your coffee this morning? We don't have any moose in eastern Oregon. I'm sure it's an elk."

"See for yourself," he said.

So I peered through the binoculars, still strapped around his neck and said, "Whoa, it is a moose!"

After five minutes of jerking the binoculars back and forth until Mike complained of binocular strap burn around his neck, a common ailment with married ranchers, we watched as the moose, growing tired of the cows, stretched out his long legs and nonchalantly stepped over the fence.

The cows, of course, stood in amazement as they watched the moose trot off into the hills. They didn't say so, but I'm sure they were in awe of an animal that didn't have to squirt through the barbed wires scratching his back, run for a gate inadvertently left open or make a group tackle on a fence post to escape. I've noticed the last few days the cows have been doing more leg stretching exercises.

Mike and I decided to jump in the pickup and see if we could track this long-legged gangly critter down to prove his existence. Stories like this are much more plausible if you have a picture.

Of course we took our trusty hunting dog, Puddin' Head. She's not very good at duck hunting, and she can't heel a cow, so we figured maybe she's a moose dog. As we drove around through the back hills and repeatedly asked her,

"Where's the moose? Find "Bullwinkle," we soon discovered she is more interested in Bullwinkle's sidekick "Rocky." Every time she saw a squirrel, she bounded around in the cab of the pickup slobbering and clawing up our arms and legs in her excitement.

We never did see Bullwinkle again, but several others in our area have reported moose sightings, making it possible to tell our story without suffering the backlash of unbelievers. I know it's a small thing, but since we don't live close enough to Mount St. Helens to watch it erupt, and hurricane Ivan completely missed us, we will always have our moose to talk about.

Let me tell ya, I've been to the other side of the fence, and the grass ain't no greener.

Caution, Slippery
When Wet

It was a dark and stormy night, but then it's always a dark and stormy night when cows are having trouble calving. Heaven forbid they should give birth to a breech calf or a 150-pound mammoth baby on a nice sunny afternoon!

A cow could be straining for an hour, and when you go out to check her in good weather, she will stop and walk away nonchalantly whistling as if everything is O.K. And if she knows she is going to have problems, she will actually cross her legs and hold that calf in until nightfall, and then only try to have it if she senses a blizzard approaching.

So, as I was saying, it was a dark and stormy night around 9 p.m. The wind was blowing hard and the skies had chosen this night to dump a month's worth of rain all at once.

In the middle of this outburst of Mother Nature, my husband, Mike, and I went out to check a cow that an hour before had looked like she was getting ready to calve.

As soon as the cows heard the four-wheeler coming, they scattered, similar to the balls on a pool table after a break, into all four corners. Only, unlike the pool balls, the cows kept shuffling around, exchanging positions making it hard with a spotlight to tell which ones we had already looked at. I'm convinced they do this on purpose because I can always hear them snickering amongst themselves on these occasions.

Once we found the cow that's trying to have a baby, there was, as always, a little group of interested cows hovering around her watching. To see what's going on we had to go in and break it up like detectives on a crime scene, "Nothing here to see girls, move along now. Go on back to your corners and graze."

So, once we got past all of their usual shenanigans, this particular cow had just given birth and was standing about 25 feet from her newborn calf watching as it struggled to get up. Thank goodness, I thought, it looks O.K., now we can go back to the house and get warm. But, as we examined the situation a little closer, something looked amiss. The calf looked like it was doing fine, but the mother hadn't bothered to lick it off as is the custom among cows.

While we were sitting on the four-wheeler in the drenching rain pondering this situation, all of a sudden the cow let out a huge bellow and stampeded toward her calf at a dead run and stopped about 12 inches short of trampling it. She then proceeded to butt it around with her head.

Now, I'm no expert, but I think this cow had been contemplating what had just happened to her, and after assessing the situation she had finally figured out the source of all her pain and was more than slightly annoyed at it. Having witnessed this type of mad cow behavior before, during their postnatal phase, we sat and watched for a few more minutes to see if she would settle down and start taking care of it.

But, seeing us huddled on the four-wheeler shivering in the shadows, I'm sure the cow decided that since she had no problems having the calf, she would take advantage of this situation anyway, like most cows would, to keep us out in the nasty weather longer. So, she proceeded to get really aggressive with the calf and acted like she was going to grind it into the mud with her head.

My husband was driving so he said, "Quick, chase her away from the calf." So I jumped off the four-wheeler and ran up to her just in time to see the glare of her eyes shimmering through the rain before she turned and started running after me.

So, I made a hasty retreat to the only nearby protection — the other side of the four-wheeler where Mike was still sitting. After tiring of watching the circus of me running circles around him with the cow in hot pursuit, Mike finally stepped off the four-wheeler between me and the cow, and in a very calm, but demanding tone said, "Git out of here you old bitty."

There was a brief moment of indecision as the cow and I both stopped and looked at each other wondering which one of us he was referring to. I finally said, "I think he means you sister, so scoot!" She reluctantly turned and shuffled off to join the cow congregation that had now gathered to watch the evening's events.

"What in the heck were you doing?" Mike said.

"Well, wasn't it obvious?" I said. "I was using myself as a decoy to lure her away from her calf!"

Not wanting to witness another raging female that night, he offered encouragingly, "Well, I guess it kind of worked."

With the cow out of the way, we quickly turned our attention to the calf that was still flaying around on the ground trying to stand up.

"We'll have to get the calf into the barn and then go get the cow and bring her in and milk her and see if we can get this little guy fed," Mike said.

He instructed me to get on the back of the four-wheeler — of course that's where ranch wives always ride when the dog isn't along — and he maneuvered the slimy, wet calf onto the rack behind me. I grabbed one of his legs on each side of me and wrapped him around my waist like a rather large fanny pack as Mike steered us to the barn.

The barn is on the other side of the corrals so Mike dropped the calf and me off in front of the corral gate and said, "Get him into the barn and I'll go get the cow."

No problem...or so I thought. I leaned over to pick up the 80-pound calf by wrapping my arms around his chest and he immediately proceeded to squirt out of my hands. He was so slimy and slippery from the birth and the rain that I couldn't hang on to him. So I tried picking him up by hanging on a little lower around his middle, and the same thing happened — he slid right down to the ground. I even tried picking him up upside down by his rump first, and that didn't do either one of us any favors, in fact, when he slid down this time I went with him. Every time I just about got him picked up and would take a step or two toward the barn, he would shoot out of my hands like a big fish.

After about 10 minutes of this, I was covered in slime and mud, and was wet from head to toe, and had only made about 20 feet of progress in my quest for the barn.

I finally had to stop and rest, and while I was waiting to catch my breath, Mike, who was nearing the corrals with the cow yelled, "You did know that he could probably walk by now didn't you?"

"Errrr, yeah...sure, I was just getting ready to let him do that," I said as I turned and lifted the calf to a standing position.

"O.K. little guy," I said to the calf, "let's get you in the barn." He just stood there. I nudged him with my knees; he still just stood there. I pushed and lifted on his rump, which immediately went up into the air while he braced his front legs in the locked position.

"Alright, if that's the way you want it," I told the calf, "I'll use your hind legs and steer you like a wheelbarrow." I soon found out that trying to pick up a slimy calf's hind legs and hold onto them when he was now old enough to offer some resistance, isn't much easier than trying to pick up the whole slimy calf.

After several attempts, I finally threw up my arms in disgust and said, "That's it, I give up. You can just stay out here." I turned and started to walk toward the barn thinking that I would at least open the doors for Mike to get the cow in, when I went about 10 steps and heard this faint little moo. I looked over my shoulder and the calf was following me.

"Nah," I told myself, "it couldn't be this easy." So I took a few more steps and the calf came running up behind me again. "We'll I'll be darned," I said, "it looks like you finally decided to cooperate." In the process, he had apparently also decided out of desperation that I was his only hope at getting some food and he started butting me. Fortunately he wasn't old enough to do much damage, and he eventually butted me all the way into the barn.

About that time, the cow, with Mike following, came bursting into the barn. I was standing in a corner of the barn and had nowhere to go to get out of her way, so I clenched my body preparing for the worst and waited for her to take her frustration out on me. She came right up to me and sniffed my coat, which was covered in calf slime, and began licking me. Feeling a little uncomfortable with this sudden show of affection, especially after our earlier encounter, I shoved the calf that had been standing behind me in front of her nose and she started licking him instead. Apparently she was no longer mad at the little guy.

"Just wait till he becomes a teenager," I told her, "and you'll be mad all over again."

The Handyman vs. the Handyma'am

I've always considered myself pretty handy around the house as far as taking care of minor plumbing problems, vacuum cleaner repairs, and putting up shelves. Not so much because I really enjoy this type of work, but because I've learned over the years that if you ask a man to do it, you are looking at a minimum of three weeks before you see any results.

For instance, if you ask your husband to hang a painting on the wall you should allow for, at the very least, four straight days of nagging him to do it. Then, it will take a good week of him complaining about your nagging and reiterating how he never has any time to just sit and relax (mainly because he is spending all of his time complaining about your nagging). After that's settled, it takes at least another week for the guilt to set in and maybe even a call from his mother before any action is taken.

When the big day finally arrives the tool belt comes out with several different gadgets attached because no job around the house can be performed by a man without a minimum of five tools, and it usually takes more. And keep in mind, this is not a good time to say, "For crying out loud all I want is a nail in the wall," or you may never get that painting out of the closet and into view.

The first thing he always asks you is where you want the painting. Having had three weeks to mull this over you have a pretty good idea and tell him exactly where you would like to see it. But you probably won't get it there because he wouldn't want to put a 1/2-inch nail into a weight-bearing wall for fear of compromising the integrity of the entire house. Besides, it might interfere with his ability to recline the Lay-Z-Boy should he ever decide to move it to that wall. Or later you may find that the real reason is because that is the exact spot he had planned on hanging that impressive life-size fuzzy velvet portrait of five dogs of various breeds sitting at a table playing poker.

Once the "correct" place is finally selected for the painting, the stud finder comes out of the tool belt. After 10 minutes of him placing the stud finder on himself and saying, "Oh look, it found me!" he finally puts it on the wall only to discover your house was built without the use of studs. This is a real turning point in the project and careful planning on the wife's part will determine whether or not he will continue with it. Upon further inspection the wife finds that he drained the batteries playing with the stud finder and pulls out spare batteries from her emergency stash.

Once it is determined that there is indeed a stud in the room, other than the one hanging the painting, out comes the measuring tape. There are few things that men like to do more than measuring. In fact, while trying to talk your husband into doing a job like this, it's a good idea to get out his tape measure and entice him with it before hand.

First the painting is measured on all sides to determine if the creator of the frame was off one-thousandth of an inch, which could throw the entire project out of whack. Then the room is measured from floor to ceiling and from end to end to find the exact center of the wall, Unfortunately, that doesn't coincide with any of the studs he found so he decides to measure himself and see how tall he is now. This leads to a trip to the bathroom to weigh himself and then to the kitchen for that leftover lasagna.

Again, the prudent wife will get out the measuring tape, which no man can resist, and entice him back to the job. Once the perfect spot is calculated he places a small dot on the wall with a pencil. At this point the wife would be really tempted to say "Don't you need to mark it a little larger so you can find it again?" but please refrain, this could shut down the entire project. Once he comes back from getting his cordless drill and discovers this for himself, he will undoubtedly say that he needs to recalculate the "perfect spot" again to make sure his figures are correct.

The pull of the tape measure is just too strong and he may go through the measuring process several times before actually performing the work. If he starts coming toward you with the measuring tape, this is the perfect time to get him that piece of banana cream pie you have been saving and offer it to him.

After the lengthy drill bit selection, which has to be the perfect size for the perfect nail, which took considerable time to choose from his four tier nail bin, he is finally ready to make a hole in the wall. This has to be done with great care as the drill hole has to be perfectly straight and not tilted to one side or the other even a fraction of an inch or the husband will have to exhibit his puttying skills. So, this is a good time to hold your breath and hope for the best.

Once the hole is drilled to his satisfaction, the nail is hammered in with a special dual head non-rebounding hammer. After inspecting his work he goes back to the kitchen for the rest of the lasagna.

This is another crucial point in the project. If you want to see your painting make it to the wall do everything you can to prevent him from turning the T.V. on to the sports channel. Even though he will tell you he can watch it and do the work at the same time, don't fall for this ploy. Put on a negligee, perform the rumba, and get out the Karaoke machine if you have to, but don't let him touch the T.V.

Once he places the painting on the nail, then he needs to get out the level. Leveling the painting could take some time, not because it's difficult, but because men become fascinated with watching that little bubble to see if they can move the level across the entire top of the painting without it moving. In fact, if video game manufacturers could come up with a game that requires the player to put the bubble in the center, every man in America would own one.

You may think at this point the job is done, but then comes the two days of bragging about his work when you show your family, friends, neighbors — even the dog — what a good job he did, because at some point you may want him to do something else around the house.

So as you can see, asking a man to hang a painting is a very long-term project and the reason why a lot of women become handy around the house. If a woman were to hang a painting she would select a wall, grab a nail out of a rusty coffee can, pound it in the wall with a rock, shoe, T.V. remote, or whatever is available and hang the picture by eyeballing it.

But one word of caution, if you decide to be the do-it-yourself wife, don't ever let him see you using a table knife as a screwdriver. I've noticed this can send them into a frenzy.

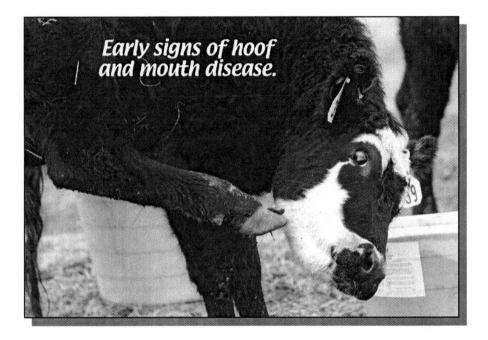

Early signs of hoof
and mouth disease.

The Magic of Ranching

A friend and co-worker recently loaned me a DVD about the life and work of Siegfried & Roy, the famous magicians and animal tamers. This dazzling duo had performed on the Las Vegas strip with their rare white tigers for nearly 30 years until 2003 when Roy was injured on stage by one of the big cats.

It got me to thinking though; ranchers are really not much different from magicians and animal tamers. For instance, Siegfried & Roy could make an animal or person disappear with the use of props, i.e. boxes and capes, and then make them reappear. Heck, ranchers do this all the time and without the props. All he has to do is announce that it's time to fix the fences and his wife and kids will magically disappear. As soon as branding is over, tah dah…they reappear.

Magicians have always been famous for pulling a rabbit out of their hats, but I believe we have them beat when it comes to this trick. You leave a hat in the barn long enough and you'll be able to pull out rabbits, mice, birds, and even the occasional skunk. And the latter animal gives the rancher the added benefit of being able to mysteriously make everyone's eyes in the audience water and their noses burn all at the same time. Now see if Siegfried & Roy can do that!

Making money disappear is really easy for ranchers. No sooner than we get it in our hands the banks and feed supply stores magically take it away. Now you see it – now you don't.

Then there's the trick where magicians magically pull something out of your ear. That's no amazing feat — at any given time you can pull a strand of straw, a stem of hay, or about two pounds of dirt out of a rancher's ear.

Ranchers can train horses to do tricks that mimic stage performances with little or no effort. For instance, when a rancher is out in the pasture gathering cattle on a horse, the horse will perform amazing acrobatic feats by bucking, hopping, and twisting with no provocation or cuing from the rancher whatsoever. They will also stand up on their hind legs like the infamous Lone Ranger's Silver and spin in a half circle and run at lightning speed toward the barn.

One of their favorite tricks is to make the rancher disappear. This feat is done by having the horse walk as close to the fence, or any protruding structure as he can and literally swipe the rancher off his back. Sometimes ranchers train their horses to do these tricks so well that the rancher himself is often surprised when the horse decides to perform these feats of his own accord. Of course, horses won't perform these tricks without a good-sized audience of friends and neighbors present and it's important for ranchers to hide their surprise and act like they cued the horse to perpetuate the illusion of his amazing ability to train horses.

Ranchers also tame cows much like the traditional lion tamers. Like lions, cows are somewhat limited by what they will do for you in the way of performing, but you can teach them to do the standard tricks.

For instance, you can stick your hand in a cow's mouth like they do with lions or even your head if you wear a grass wig and have something handy to mop up the slobber. Unlike lions though that you can whip at to get to jump through hoops or paw the air and roar, cows will react differently to these cues. If you whip at a cow's backside she will turn around and plow you over. If you whip at a cow's head, she will plow you over without turning around. And if you whip at a cow's feet, she will without a doubt kick you. Although these may not be the desired responses, they can be quite entertaining.

Even though you can't teach a cow to stand on a large ball without flattening it, audiences seem to be just as impressed by the cow tamer's ability to produce fertilizer from the cow's backside throughout the entire act. And unlike magicians, ranchers will almost always let those in the audience who come prepared with containers take home a "little souvenir."

Up until now, most magic shows performed by ranchers have taken place in the barnyards and pastures, but I would really like to see a rancher take his magic show to the Las Vegas strip like "Siegfried & Roy — Masters of the Impossible." I can just see it now — the neon sign outside of the Mirage lit up in the night with the headliner: "The Amazing Vern Farfuss and His Common Cows — Masters of Manure."

Sure, we can have dinner out, I'll just move the trough outside!

Mother's Day — A Day
for Mothers and Wives

Mother's Day is one of those complicated holidays — it can make a woman cry, make her laugh and even incite anger — similar to puberty, weddings, birth, menopause, birthdays and every other important day in a woman's life. And it doesn't even have to be her special day – it can be someone else's.

Since husbands don't know which one of these three reactions, that to them seemingly arrive randomly like lottery winnings, to expect from their wives, they often times start getting flinchy a few days before the event. They start ducking at the slightest movement in case an airborne frying pan is coming their way. They choose their words very carefully or to be safe, they don't talk at all; and oftentimes the stress becomes so intense that they just disappear for a few days prior to the big day, returning just in time for the celebration with the belief that their wives surely wouldn't make a big scene in front of other family members and friends. And that's where they make their first mistake. If a big scene is in order, we will make it in front of anyone, anywhere, anytime!

And men, I've noticed, don't always learn from previous mistakes that they make with their wives. Instead, they think this year will be different because their wife, based on past years, won't be expecting anything special this year — wrong! We think that based on past years, you should know better this year and plan accordingly.

So, for this Mother's Day here is a word of advice to husbands: If you're getting vibes that maybe you should do something special for the mother of your children, even though you rationalize that "your wife is not 'your' mother" (and by the way saying that will definitely get you the frying pan and the unwanted anger reaction followed by the unwanted crying reaction, after which you will have to buy something really nice to get the desired laughing response) then by all means do something special. And while you're at it, don't forget the other most important woman in your life — your own mother.

Kids have it a little easier though. I remember when my son, now 21, was about 8 years old. On Mother's Day he looked up at me with his big blue eyes and I thought he was going to say something really special and meaningful to me. Instead, he said, "Mommy, shouldn't Mother's Day be a day where mommies are so happy to have kids that they buy them lots of presents?"

However, while a cute incident like this from young children can incite the laughter reaction in mothers, husbands shouldn't expect the same results if they try cute phases instead of dinner and flowers on their wives.

In a husband's defense though, young kids have an advantage — teachers usually have their students make something special in class for them to present to their mothers. So, on this special day I would like to thank all of you teachers who remember everyone's mother on Mother's Day, even though we are not "your" mothers.

One thing that makes Mother's Day so special is that mothers always feel a great sense of respect and love for their own mothers on this day. I know with my mother, Mother's Day is a time that I reflect on the many wonderful things she has done for me, the advice and comfort she as given me over the years, and it's also the day that I go to her and beg her to take off the "curse."

She placed the curse on me when I was about 16 years old during one of those special mother-daughter talks, following an episode where I had brought her car home with the entire side dented in. After grounding me for life, she said, "When you grow up, I hope you have a kid just like you!"

At the time I just laughed if off, but as my son approached his teenage years, I realized a mother's curse was a formidable power that shouldn't be taken lightly. And now that he is a young man, once again as this special day approaches, I beg you, "Please Mom, take off the curse already!"

For all of you mothers, grandmothers, and special women who take on the roles of nurturing our children, and my own very special mother, I thank you and wish you a wonderful day full of the best reaction of all – much love.

And for all of you husbands — remember — Father's Day is just around the corner...not that we wives are a vengeful lot, but why take any chances!

No son, for the 100th time, when a cow laughs, milk does not come out her nose.

Yucking It up on the Ranch

After a 50-hour week at work I came home last Friday night about 8 p.m. exhausted. Following a quick dinner I went to bed with instructions to my husband, Mike, not to wake me until noon Saturday, and then only if the house was burning down and for some reason he couldn't pack the bed out with me in it.

So I was less than shall we say "polite" when at 9:30 p.m. I was awakened by a familiar sound.

"Deeeeeear.....I have something for you," he yelled from downstairs.

"What?" I snapped, "for your sake I hope the house is fully engulfed!"

"It's a surprise, come look," he continued.

I managed to crawl out of bed and look over the stair railing and there he stood with a wet black bundle under each arm dripping into slime puddles on the floor.

"It's twins!" he exclaimed.

The only way to describe a calf in those first moments, when it comes out of a cow, is "yucky." They appear to have the makings of a 24-egg omelet smeared into their hairy little hides. In most cases their moms can look past the goo and give them a proper cleaning; however, I have seen more than a few take one look and run the other way. I tried that the first couple of times I was asked to be a surrogate mother to one of these slimy little creatures, but like with the cows, my husband tracked me down and made me come back.

"All right," I conceded, "get them into the bathroom."

It was a really cold and stormy evening and the calves, being so small and weak, were too cold to stand, so the first priority was to get them dried off and warm.

I threw a tarp on the floor that we keep handy for just such an emergency and Mike one by one let them slide out of his arms onto it. With a small floor heater, two blow driers, and an electric heating pad going, the room very quickly became a 105-degree calf incubator.

Keep in mind that our bathroom is pretty small and take into account, with the enamel fixtures and shower, there is only about six feet of floor space left. The sprawled out calves took up about four and half feet of the space, so as we worked on warming the calves and drying them with towels and the afore mentioned blow driers, Mike and I maneuvered over the last foot and a half of floor space straddling the calves like playing a game of Twister. Right foot to white-faced calf's left ear, left hand to green toilet seat (lid closed of course)…And then there was the occasional, "eeeew, I just got my hand in something gooey — make way – I've got to get to the sink."

When calves are this cold and wet it takes considerable time and lots of towels to dry them off before they show signs of life. Finally, after more than two hours of drying, the calves were sitting upright, and as the clock in the next room chimed midnight, our patience and our backs were on their last legs.

We wrestled around for another half hour getting some milk, which Mike had extracted from the not so willing cow earlier, down them and decided they were in good shape for the night.

As we stood and surveyed the slime-strewn room, I silently pointed to the pile of yucky, soaked towels on the floor.

"What?" he said.

"Can you please pick them up?" I asked.

"Why can't you pick them up?" he said.

"You're closer to them," I replied.

He stepped back a few inches, "Not any more!"

Which in turn, I stepped back two inches. "Oh yes, I think you are," I said.

We kept stepping back a few inches at a time until we had climbed over the calves and were at opposite ends of the bathroom against the walls, which isn't very far apart in such a small room. We glared at each other like two gunfighters in a cheap western movie, both waiting for the other to "reach for it," and pick up the towels.

My arm twitched and I leaned forward slightly, and immediately retracted when I saw the smile of satisfaction spread across his face. After a few more minutes he sighed and shifted his weight to bend over. I thought, "I have him now he's going in for the towels." No such luck, he merely bent over to scratch his leg.

Finally, the standoff ended when one of the calves struggled into a standing position and bawled.

"Oh look," I exclaimed, "they're going to be O.K."

At that point I would like to say that also, similar to the movies, our eyes met, our souls touched, and we walked out of the bathroom smiling hand in hand, but at 1 a.m. who has the energy for such nonsense? Instead, we continued to battle over who was going to pick up the towels for another 10 minutes, until we decided to each pick up half and then went our separate ways to get cleaned up and ready for bed.

We fell into bed grumbling and complaining about sore knees, strained backs and lack of sleep, only to wake up two hours later to check the heifers. But you know, I wouldn't trade this lifestyle for anything, because contrary to the way calves look when they are first born, once dried off and de-slimed, they are about the cutest little critters God ever created. I just need to keep reminding myself of that every time I step into or put my hand into something yucky....

Care to Tango?

The Bleeping Beep Beep

After a full day of mending fences, my muscles were sore, my hands were blistered, and I was dog-tired. Not the kind of tired like a snoozing dog who keeps one ear flap open and an alert snout to sniff the evening breeze for dead rodents, but the Puddin' Head kind of tired.

After Puddin' Head, our black Lab, Chihuahua, St. Bernard, and Lord only knows what cross, spends the day chasing the four-wheeler, tractor, grasshoppers, or anything else that has the unfortunate side affect of moving, she lies flat on her back. Her legs are sprawled in all directions, her mouth gapes open, and her tongue hits the floor and rolls out like a fly strip waiting for insects to adhere to it. For all practical purposes she's dead to the world. Not a very pretty sight, but I don't care. That's how tired I was – Puddin' Head tired.

As soon as my head hit the pillow, I assumed the position. It would have been a good time for a grizzly bear to

111

pay a visit because I could have won an Oscar for playing dead. Nothing, not an earthquake, aerial attack of killer tomatoes or buckets of ice water to the face would have woke me — if it hadn't been for that blasted beep.

The first couple of beeps I heard, I easily incorporated into my dream: You want me to pitch how much of that beep beep hay into those beep beep feed bunks for your beep beep cows! (I know it's getting close to winter when I start having feeding dreams.) But, alas, there are only so many beeps you can use in a dream before you realize that they are coming from somewhere beyond your sleep realm.

"What's that beeping?" I asked, as I nudged my husband, Mike, in the ribs.

"It's your cell phone," he said groggily, "go shut it off."

So, I trudged down the stairs, got my cell phone out of my purse, and ended its connection with the world for the night. I just got back upstairs and when my head hit the pillow, we heard it again – beep beep.

"It must be your cell phone," I told Mike. It was then his turn to go downstairs and hit the power off button to his yak box and say "cell ya later" to would be callers.

O.K., now back to the business of sleeping…. beep beep. Can the cell phones make a noise when they are turned off, we wondered… Just then Mike said, "I know, it's got to be a dead battery in one of the smoke alarms." He stomped back down the stairs, and pretty soon I heard chairs moving and plastic popping along with a few swear words as he proceeded to disconnect every alarm in the house.

Back in bed again, he said, "There, that should take care of it."

Beep beep….

"That wasn't it," I said.

That prompted a mass search by both of us. We turned off all the digital clocks in the house, and checked the microwave, the oven, the stereo, T.V., computer, VCR, dishwasher, clothes dryer, and even Puddin' Head who of course was still asleep during all of this.

After we were satisfied that we had turned off and unplugged everything electronic in the house, we went back to bed...only to be serenaded by the bleeping beep beep again.

"It almost sounds like it's coming from outside," I said. "I wonder if it's my car?"

Mike flew out of bed and went outside to investigate the new Subaru that I had purchased just a couple of days before. A few minutes later he came back in and reported that there was a light on in my car, which might be making the noise and that I needed to figure out how to turn it off.

So, we were both outside circling my car like a couple of sleep-deprived, pajama-clad burglars peeping in the windows trying to figure out what the lit-up button said. Every time we opened the car door the light went off and it couldn't be read.

"Maybe if we get in and close the doors, it will light up again," I said.

As we were both sitting in the front seats of my Subaru, we discovered the red light said, "Security."

"Well, turn it off," said Mike, "so we can get some sleep."

"I don't know how to turn it off," I said, as I grabbed the owner's manual out of the jockey box.

Just as I found the section that said, "The security indicator light deters potential thieves by indicting that the vehicle is equipped with an immobilizer system," and was reading it out loud, Mike said, "What's this button do?" and pushed it. He set off the car alarm and the horn began honking and the lights began flashing. The security light may deter thieves, but apparently not sleepy ranchers.

I began feverously flipping through the manual trying to find how to turn that commotion off. This is one of those moments where you thank the good Lord that you are a rancher and live out in the country away from neighbors who can't see you sitting in your car at 1 a.m. in your pajamas with the alarm going off.

After about three ear-splitting minutes, I found how to turn it off in the manual, which by the way isn't set up in an easy to read format for the cranky and sleep deprived. I may have to alert Subaru to that issue.

Finally, we got everything turned off, went back into the house, tripped over the dog who was still sprawled out on the floor asleep, and crawled back into bed.

"You know, I never did hear the car make that beep beep sound while we were out there, did you? I asked. "Maybe that's not what was making the noise."

Just then, somewhere off in the distance, as I was about to doze off, I heard a faint, lone coyote howl. Puddin' Head, who had slept through horns honking, furniture moving, people stomping around cussing, and the annoying beep beep, bolted upright, sucked in her tongue, and began howling a response, which in turn got the coyote howling more.

We've learned from past experience that there is nothing we can do to get her to stop this primal exchange with a wild animal until she's darn good and ready, so we waited. In the mean time, we heard another noise... It sounded like the tone you hear when you pick up a telephone.

"What in the heck is that?" asked Mike.

"It sounds like my laptop computer is trying to connect to the Internet," I said. "Hey, I wonder if that's what's been making the beep beep noise all this time too."

Mike jumped out of bed and went tearing down the stairs.

"Where are you going?" I called after him.

"I'm not taking any chances," he said. "I'm going to put your laptop, our cell phones, and the dog in your Subaru and drive them down to the barn for the night."

A few minutes later after he returned, and as we were finally approaching slumber, I had a thought. I jabbed Mike in the ribs, "Hey, what if we have a fire? All of the alarms are disabled."

Mike sat up in bed, turned on the light, looked me directly in the eyes and said, "Do you want to join the dog in the car?"

With the proper incentive, it's amazing how fast sleep can come…

Doing the Chute Shovel and Stomp

Living in the state's Icelandic region, eastern Oregon ranchers are familiar with all kinds of snow removal devices — tractors with blades, snow blowers, four-wheelers with pieces of plywood tied on the front, and just letting visitors and the UPS driver get stuck in your driveway a few times removes some of the snow when they try to dig their way out. But the most commonly used rancher's snow removal device is a rancher's wife.

Give her a snow shovel and the right incentive and she can move a lot of snow in a short period of time. Make her mad, and she can move an entire mountain. I know, because I am one of these snow removal devices.

Last weekend my husband placed me into service digging out snow from the corral gates and the loading chute so we could take a few steers to the sale.

The main alleyway in the corrals was buried in about three feet of snow. As he saw me standing there contemplating how in the world I was going to shovel out all of that snow he came up with an idea.

"Why don't you march up and down that alley about 20 times and smash the snow down so the calves won't mind going in there," he said. "I think that will work just as well and you won't have to shovel so much."

Thus, I began my job as a combo snow removal-stomper device while he pushed snow around in the areas that were wide enough for the tractor to fit in.

I marched up and down the alley about five times and managed to make a trail that sank into the hard crusty snow about two inches deep before I heard Mike stop the tractor.

"That's not going to work," he yelled from across the corrals. "You've got to stomp harder."

"I am stomping hard," I said as I jumped up and down still bouncing off the top of the snow.

"Harder than that," he said as he came closer.

So, I stomped around some more still not making much headway.

'You've got to put your whole body into it," he said. "You're not trying hard enough."

I was getting pretty irritated at this point, partly because I wasn't making any progress, and mostly because ranch wives, as ranchers will attest, don't particularly like being told what to do. So, I mustered up all of my strength, jumped into the air, and did a full body slam just like I'd seen them do on Saturday night wrestling and I fell through the top layer of snow all the way to the bottom.

"That's it," he said. "Now just keep doing that all the way down the alley until you have it smashed down."

About an hour and 20 body slams later, I was too tired to go on and didn't have even a quarter of the snow smashed down yet. The jumping up and slamming myself down in the snow wasn't the hard part – it was the recovery time in between and crawling back up to a standing position that was wearing me out.

To make the situation worse, our black lab, Puddin' Head thought I was playing and every time I slammed down to the ground she jumped on my head.

As I was lying there flaying around in the snow like a beached whale in my insulated Carhart overalls with a dog chewing on my ears trying to get up, I heard the tractor stop again.

He walked over to me and said, "We're never going to get this done if you keep laying around playing with Puddin'," he said. "I guess I'll just have to do it myself, why don't you go shovel the snow out by the gate next to the barn."

"Great," I said rather sarcastically. "I'd like to see you do it!"

I had envisioned stomping off in a huff, but it's kind of hard when you have to roll around on the ground for five minutes to get to a place where you can even get your feet under you.

By the time I finally did get up though, I showed him. I grabbed the shovel and stomped over to the barn and began flinging snow, from the massive heap that had built up over the winter, so fast that it made his head spin Actually, I thought it had made his head spin, but he was just looking the other way and hadn't even noticed my little outburst. There's nothing worse that wasting a good tirade on someone who's not even paying attention.

I stopped shoveling snow long enough to watch and see how he had decided to handle the situation in the alleyway. He walked over and stomped around on the snow unsuccessfully for a few minutes and headed back toward the tractor.

"Ha," I yelled. "Too much for ya, huh?"

He just kept walking without saying a word and went past the tractor to the hay pile. He grabbed a large flake of hay and came back and scattered it up and down the alleyway where I had spent the better part of the morning stomping.

He then opened a gate, which led into the corral from a nearby pen that held a dozen steers. He stood back as the steers ambled into the alley and I watched while they stomped every last flake of snow down to the ground in about five minutes.

"Well, why in the heck didn't you do that before?" I asked.

"You know, I never thought of it," he said. "If I had spread out a big cheesecake in there for you, you probably would have finished the job a lot faster too."

We're a Rockin', but
We're Not Rollin'

Being a rancher's wife and living 25 miles out of town, I have had to endure all types of driving conditions — snow, sleet, ice, fog, hail, wind, and backseat drivers. (I would have placed wind and backseat drivers in the same category, but I think most vehicles are already equipped with something similar called an air bag.) So, having to drive pickups, tractors and four-wheelers in all of these types of conditions has made me pretty confident in my ability to maneuver a vehicle around in less than perfect conditions — including the foot of new snow that we received one night a few weeks ago.

As I was preparing for work the next morning my husband, Mike, asked me if he needed to plow the driveway, which is about 1/4 mile long, before he went out to feed the cattle so my son, Jake, and I could get to town.

"Nah," I said. "I can get through that, I've got four-wheel drive and I've driven through more snow than this. I've even had to walk through more snow than this to get to school as a kid, five feet to be exact...three miles of it in blinding blizzards...one time barefoot..."

"O.K., O.K.," he interrupts. "You can stop, I get your point. I'll go feed the cows and see you tonight."

With that, Jake and I hopped in my pickup and headed down the driveway...well...where I thought the drive way should be... It had snowed so much that the slopes along the sides of the driveway had filled in making the road level with the adjacent pasture and I couldn't tell where the road was.

As I was maneuvering my pickup through the snow on the non-visible road, trying to remember exactly how close the road was to the haystack, Jake broke my concentration yelling, "You're going off the road, turn your wheels!" I figured he should know because he has been telling me how to drive ever since he got his driver's license and became an expert, so I cranked the wheels hard to the right.

"No," he yelled. "The other way." So, I rotated to the left.

"No," he yelled again. "Straighten them up."

As I zigged and zagged across the road, he continued to shout directions until I came to a halt, which would have been O.K. had I intended to stop, but the pickup just wouldn't go any further. It seems that Jake's "careful" guidance and my apparent inability to follow directions landed us sideways in the irrigation ditch that runs parallel to the driveway.

I didn't have to ponder what had happened more than a split second though because Jake quickly assessed the situation for me.

"Well, you're off the road now," he said. "Didn't you hear me tell you to straighten the wheels?"

It's times like this that it's nice to have an expert driver along to tell you exactly what went wrong and it's even better when they tell you what you need to do about it.

"Just go forward and back until you get it to rocking," he said. "Once you get to rocking fast enough, the momentum will squirt you back onto the road."

"I don't know," I said cautiously. "Mike will be done feeding in a few minutes and he can just pull us out with the four-wheel drive tractor."

"Heck, I've gotten out of deeper holes than this before; just try it," he said.

Once again heeding the expertise of my insistent passenger, who assured me this technique would propel me out of the two-feet deep ditch, I did as he said.

After about 10 minutes of rockin' and not rollin', I said, "What's that smell? It smells like burning rubber."

Like Inspector Sherlock Holmes trying to solve a mystery, Jake got out and looked the situation over. "Well," he said, "The tires are starting to smoke a little...they're probably cheap ones or they wouldn't have gotten this hot from spinning out...I guess I better go get Mike's diesel truck and a chain," he said as he was walking back toward the house.

Since my side of the pickup was buried in the snow and my door wouldn't open, I decided it was pointless to remind him that Mike would be coming up the driveway with the tractor in a few minutes. But, just as I was pondering this possibility I looked down the hill where Mike was feeding and noticed that all of the calves that had been weaned a few weeks ago had escaped and were running into the pasture where the cows were.

I thought about going back to the house to get my boots and help him out, but about that time Jake had showed up with Mike's truck.

Jake hooked a chain between the trucks and gave me instructions to keep the wheels of my pickup straight, put it in reverse and floorboard it, while he pulled me out. So, at the same time we simultaneously pushed the pedal to the metal and Jake shot down the driveway like a rocket cleared for take off. He almost made it back to the house before he noticed that

A Rancher's Resolve...

With the beginning of the new year, I decided like many people that I would write down my New Year's resolutions. My first resolution is to stop procrastinating. Unfortunately, I haven't gotten around to writing it down yet....

It did get me to thinking though that other ranchers may not have taken the time to write down theirs yet either, so if one of the resolutions floating around in your head is to spend more time thinking about this kind of important stuff, but you have the afore mentioned affliction of procrastination, here are some suggestions you might consider:

You can resolve:

• To not cuss at the cows when they won't go up the chute, through the gate or into the corrals or anywhere else you would like them to go. Instead, say, "Come on mamas, move your $!#@s." Err...let me try that again, "Git, git up there you son of a !$@#%es." Maybe, "Hup, hup now girls, move your sorry no good $#$@&% behinds." Well, I can see that this is one resolve that is just not going to be possible so let's move on to the next one...

• To remember to call the neighbor at least 30 days after his best bull gets into your cow pasture.

• To only get your own "extra" irrigation water at night and turn it back into the ditch before morning to avoid upsetting the neighbors.

• To not knock people over rushing to get the middle seat of the pickup to avoid having to open gates. Instead, politely shove them aside and tell them you would like to give them the honor of having the window seat.

• To splurge and buy an inflatable round donut cushion for every tractor and piece of farming equipment you own, to avoid the strange looks you get from wearing it attached to your behind with baling twine during haying season.

• To retire your 10-year-old pair of frayed, holey, cow-poopie Carhartt overalls and matching jacket and buy some new ones. And that doesn't mean hanging the old ones in the closet for a "special occasion."

• To stop rolling around on the floor, clutching your chest, and gasping for air when the fertilizer bill is presented to you.

• To stop investing money in expensive stock dogs and having the barn cats vaccinated. Because the minute you pay for a dog or spend even one dollar on a cat they immediately have a religious experience and become one with the tractor tire.

• To stop asking the kids every time they leave the door open, "What, do you live in a barn?" like that would be a bad thing because at some point during their teenage years you may want them to go live in the barn.

• To start looking at cow pies as a form of economic development when they make contact with the bottom of your boots.

• To organize your "precious metals" pile so that tractor junk is in one section, baler junk has its own pile, etc., and don't forget to create a pile for miscellaneous scrap that you have no idea where it came from or what it's for, but feel that you might need it some day, "in a pinch." Who knows, that brand new shiny computerized tractor may just need a rusty old piece of deteriorating metal in its carburetor some day to keep it going.

• To put your fatter cows on a diet so when they step on your foot or knock you down and give your back a Swedish hoof massage, you won't mind so much.

• To give your 4-wheeler a break and ride your horse at least once this year. Then, when people wonder why you are walking so funny, don't admit that you are sore, say, "What do you mean, funny? This is how all "real" cowboys walk."

• And, to not cry when the Canadian market opens up to export beef into the U.S. Instead, buy a small piece of property in Canada, ship your calves to it and then export them back to the U.S. again. It's called "inside-out trading."

About The Author

Debby Schoeningh and her husband, Mike, live at the base of the Elkhorn Mountains in rural Eastern Oregon where they have a cow/calf operation.

Her writing and photography have appeared in the Western Horseman magazine, the *Oregon Business Magazine* and the *Cascade Cattleman*. She continues to contribute to several publications on a regular basis including the *Ruralite* magazine and the *Capital Press* newspaper. She is also a writer/editor at *The Record-Courier* newspaper where she writes her column "The Country Side." "The Horseless Rancher" is her second book.

Debby enjoys the beauty of nature and spends her spare time photographing the ranching life and Eastern Oregon's landscape. Her work can be seen on the Internet at http://www.thecountrysidepress.com.

The ends are in sight...

The Horseless RANCHER

Published by

The Country Side Press

P.O. Box 34
Haines, OR 97833
www.thecountrysidepress.com

Other books by The Country Side Press
"Tails From The Country Side"
By Debby Schoeningh

Printed in the United States
63282LVS00005B/310-465